HEARTS

OFFICIAL

ALL-TIME
GREATS

RODDY MACKENZIE

g

Lomond Books

A Grange Publication

© 1999

g Published by Grange Communications Ltd., Edinburgh, under licence from Heart of Midlothian Football Club.

Printed in the EU.

Photographs supplied by D. C. Thomson & Co. Ltd.

ISBN: 1-84204-003-0

CONTENTS

INTRODUCTION	5	ALEX MASSIE	51
ANDY ANDERSON	7	JOHN ROBERTSON	52
ALAN ANDERSON	8	ALFIE CONN	55
ISAAC BEGBIE	10	JOHN CUMMING	58
JOHN COLQUHOUN	11	BOB MERCER	62
BARNEY BATTLES	14	ALEX YOUNG	63
GILLES ROUSSET	16	GARY LOCKE	64
JIM CRUICKSHANK	18	ALEX MACDONALD	67
WALTER KIDD	20	GARY MACKAY	68
PERCY DAWSON	22	DREW BUSBY	71
JOHNNY HAMILTON	23	WILLIE BAULD	72
COLIN CAMERON	24	GORDON MARSHALL	75
JACK HARKNESS	27	HENRY SMITH	76
CRAIG LEVEIN	28	BOBBY WALKER	78
BOBBY KIRK	31	ALAN JOHNSTON	79
JIMMY MURRAY	32	PAUL RITCHIE	80
WILLIE HAMILTON	34	JIMMY WARDHAUGH	82
PADDY CROSSAN	35	STEVE FULTON	85
DAVIE HOLT	36	TOMMY WALKER	86
DONALD FORD	37	STEPHANE ADAM	89
DAVE McPHERSON	40	BOBBY PARKER	90
DAVE MACKAY	42	ALAN McLAREN	92
SANDY CLARK	45	THOMAS FLOGEL	93
TOMMY JENKINSON	46	BATTLES & MURRAY	94
TOM PURDIE	47	WILLIE BAULD WITH CUP	95
JIM JEFFERIES	48	NEIL McCANN & DAVID WEIR	96
WILLIE WALLACE	50		

INTRODUCTION

Many great players have worn the maroon of Heart of Midlothian since the club was formed back in 1874. A list would be almost endless as any supporter would come up with a different selection and this book is no more than an attempt to rekindle old flames and bring players together who have featured prominently in the development of the club.

Few will dispute the contribution made to Hearts by the likes of Bobby Walker, Tommy Walker, Willie Bauld and John Robertson. These are players who have become almost synonymous with the club.

Bobby Walker was perhaps the first player to gain Hearts some recognition out of Scotland and, even today, he is regarded by some as the finest player to have played for the club.

Tommy Walker was a rare breed who commanded respect both on and off a football field. Tales of his sportsmanship were legendary and, in these modern days when winning seems to be everything, he possessed the true spirit of sport. He is almost as fondly remembered in London for his brief stint at Chelsea as he is around Tynecastle.

As was the case with John Robertson some years later, he could not resist the pulling power of Hearts and returned to the club after a sojourn in English football. Robertson, the modern-day "King of Hearts", had only a brief spell at Newcastle United before he retraced his footsteps and his goal touch had not deserted him along the way as he went on to beat Jimmy Wardhaugh's great league goal-scoring record for the club.

And what of Willie Bauld? He is still talked about in reverential terms and, even if he was given scant international recognition by the Scotland selectors, it has not detracted from the legend.

Other players in this book may not have scaled the same heights but all of them have served their time with distinction. From Tom Purdie - the first captain of Hearts - to Colin Cameron, the most recent keeper of the captain's armband, there have been heroes aplenty.

Maybe Alex MacDonald and Jim Jefferies will be remembered more for their managerial merits than playing prowess - MacDonald having taken Hearts from the first division to the brink of a Premier League and Scottish Cup double and Jefferies having ended a 36-year trophy famine - but their commitment to the Hearts' cause can never be doubted.

As the club enters a new century, it is as good a time as any to take stock of players who have lit up the past and some who promise to ignite the future.

There will inevitably be supporters who feel some players who have been omitted should have been included ahead of others. That is a matter for healthy debate.

What is without dispute is that the players listed in the pages ahead built Hearts into what they are today. The memories live on.

ANDY ANDERSON

But for Bobby Walker, Andy Anderson would have been Hearts' most-capped player. Walker received 29 caps for Scotland, just half a dozen more than Anderson and although, in the modern era, Dave McPherson won 27 international caps, many of those were when he was with Rangers.

Anderson, a tough-tackling full-back, played at Tynecastle for eleven years after signing from junior side, Baillieston, in September, 1929. He made his debut in January, 1930 and made the right-back berth his own during the thirties.

He was the best right-back of his generation and was soon an automatic choice for Scotland, even going on to captain his country after making his Scotland debut against England at the age of 24 in April, 1933, in a 2-1 win at Hampden.

Brother-in-law of Jock White, who was a popular Tynecastle forward in the 1920s and who had been Hearts' record signing at the time.

Anderson gained a reputation as a rugged and reliable defender and he went on to play over 450 games for Hearts before retiring from the game in 1940, with Hearts his only senior club.

Born: Airdrie, 1909.
Signed from: Baillieston.
Debut: January, 1930.
Appearances: 475.

ALAN ANDERSON

Born and brought up in Leith, Alan Anderson's allegiance from an early age was not to Hibernian but to Hearts. As a supporter of the club, he always wanted to play for Hearts but his route to Tynecastle was a circuitous one.

Having played for Dalkeith Thistle, it was Falkirk who gave him his first senior break but his next port of call was south of the border, at Millwall, where he stayed for three years and helped the team win the Fourth Division title in 1962.

From there, the towering centre-half was sold to Scunthorpe United for £10,000 but he lasted there only four months before returning to Scotland to sign for Hearts for a knock-down £1,500 in November, 1963.

It was money well spent, as the popular defender went on to play over 500 games for the club and for a centre-half, scored more than his fair share of valuable goals.

Noted for his power in the air and his ability to read the game, Anderson was an ever-present in the Hearts defence in the sixties and early seventies. He made his debut on January 2, 1964, in a 2-1 win over Dunfermline.

The result that hurt most that year was the 7-1 home defeat by a Charlie Cooke-inspired Dundee at the end of February. It had been totally out of character - Hearts had lost only one of their previous eight matches - and come the end of the season, it was the fact that Hearts conceded 49 goals over the season (the worst record in the top five) that was to ultimately be the downfall.

Anderson and Cruickshank were the only ever-presents in the league the following season when Hearts, perhaps understandably, dipped to seventh but by then Anderson was showing that he had an eye for goal when he went up for set-pieces.

His first goal for the club came in Europe in a 3-3 draw with Zarragoza, of Spain in the first round of the Fairs' Cup at Tynecastle. Anderson also scored in the return leg, which finished 2-2 and before the away-goals' rule, it meant a play-off in Spain, which Hearts were to lose 1-0.

Anderson was to prove himself a stalwart in the Hearts defence and went on to captain the side. He played in the 1968 Scottish Cup Final against Dunfermline (when the opposition was captained by his former defensive partner, Barry) but like Cruickshank, he was destined to leave Tynecastle without a winners' medal.

In 1971, he also played in the team that reached the Texaco Cup Final but lost over two legs to Wolves. He held onto the number five shirt until the end of 1975, when John Gallacher replaced him. He played his last game for Hearts in a 0-0 draw with St Johnstone at Muirton Park at the end of April, 1976 but never made the following match - the Scottish Cup Final defeat by Rangers at Hampden.

He retired from the game in 1976 and although he never won a full international cap, he played in representative matches for Scotland in 1966-67 against Israel, Hong Kong, Australia, Auckland Province and Canada.

Born: Edinburgh, December 21, 1939.
Signed from: Scunthorpe United.
Debut: January 2, 1964, First Division, Hearts 2 Dunfermline 1.
Appearances: 537. Goals: 37.

ISAAC BEGBIE

saac Begbie was an inspirational captain for Hearts at the end of the 19th century. Brought up close to the ground, he joined Hearts at the age of 20 in 1888 - just two years after the opening of the Tynecastle ground.

Begbie, an uncompromising wing-half, had the distinction of scoring Hearts' first league goal - against Rangers, in a 5-2 defeat on August 18, 1890.

It was a surprise result at the time and when Hearts lost their first home league game 5-0 to Celtic the following week, Begbie was one of five home players who were labelled by one local report as having "lost the ability which gained them fame."

But Begbie went on to help Hearts to the Scottish Cup in 1891 and 1896 and captained Hearts to their first league title in 1895 ,when they lost only two of their 20 matches and scored 50 goals.

He also guided the team to the title again two years later, after the great Bobby Walker had been recruited. Hearts had to beat Clyde home and away to win the title in 1897 and did so - 5-1 and 5-0 - to pip Celtic by two points.

It was to be the last league title that Hearts were to win for 61 years, when the team was managed by another Walker, Tommy.

After helping Hearts to their first Scottish Cup success in 1891 with a 1-0 win over Dumbarton in the final, he was one of only three survivors - David Russell and David Baird being the others - for the 1896 final against Hibs.

The final - the only one in the history of the competition to be played outside of Glasgow - was held at Logie Green and in front of a crowd of 16,034, Hearts won 3-1.

Begbie stood only 5'8" but his stature in the Scottish game was immense. He won four full international caps and also represented the Scottish League on three occasions.

During the latter part of his career at Tynecastle, he took Bobby Walker under his wing and helped Walker become arguably the most respected player of his generation.

Begbie went on to play more than 400 games for Hearts before he left to join Leith Athletic in 1900 and thus missed out on Hearts' third Scottish Cup win the following year.

Born: Edinburgh, 1868.
Signed from: Dalry Albert.
Appearances: 425.
International honours: Scotland (4).

JOHN COLQUHOUN

As manager of Hearts, Alex MacDonald was renowned for his ability to spot a bargain in the transfer market and there was no shrewder buy than John Colquhoun. In the second-half of the 1984-85 season, it became apparent to MacDonald that he needed to freshen up his team - Jimmy Bone, Donald Park, Willie Johnston and MacDonald, himself, all reaching the end of their playing days.

Colquhoun was one of the new faces brought in - for a bargain £50,000 from Celtic - and he was one of the players who was to figure prominently in the team that came so close to a league and cup double in 1985-86.

A winger of genuine pace and great close-control, his mobility caused numerous defenders problems. After scoring on his debut for Hearts - in a 1-1 draw with former club, Celtic, at Tynecastle - he went on to finish third-top scorer in his first season behind John Robertson and Sandy Clark.

But his eye for goal was to mark him down as a player that opponents had to watch and in 1986-87, 1987-88 and 1988-89, only Robertson managed to score more goals than him.

Colquhoun also had a knack of scoring important goals. In 1986, he scored the only goal of the Scottish Cup semi final against Dundee United at Hampden which sent Hearts into their first Scottish Cup Final for ten years.

In the memorable league campaign that year, he scored twice in a 2-0 win over Rangers at Ibrox, notched the only goal of a critical encounter at Pittodrie not long afterwards and in a televised Sunday match at Tynecastle at the end of April, snatched a vital late equaliser against Aberdeen which took Hearts to within striking distance of the title.

An uncanny ability to steer clear of injuries meant he missed few matches for Hearts over the next few seasons. He played a major role in league and cup matches and almost scored a goal to treasure in Munich in the UEFA Cup quarter final, second leg, against Bayern in 1989, when his header struck a post. Had it gone in, it would have been the goal which would have taken Hearts through on away goals.

Where Colquhoun had, like Robertson, fed off the aerial ability of Sandy Clark, Hearts were no less effective when he operated in a diminuitive front three with Robertson and the emerging Scott Crabbe. The goals continued to come and in season 1989-90, the three shared 47 between them, although, admittedly, Colquhoun was a distant third.

Colquhoun left Hearts at the end of the 1990-91 season, in which where he had been the only over-present and he joined Millwall in a £400,000 deal, as then manager, Joe Jordan, wanted money to re-shape his team. But he was to return at the end of Jordan's reign, when Sandy Clark brought him back at the start of the 1993-94 season as part of the £500,000 transfer that took Derek Ferguson to Sunderland.

Colquhoun was soon paying back his former team-mate turned manager and in addition to scoring in the UEFA Cup tie against Atletico Madrid at Tynecastle, he notched both goals in a 2-0 Edinburgh derby win over Hibs in the October.

If Colquhoun was to figure less under Tommy McLean, who succeeded Clark as manager, he had a fair first season under Jim

Jefferies when he scored seven times in 28 appearances, including the consolation strike in the 5-1 Scottish Cup Final defeat by Rangers at Hampden.

Colquhoun was then a victim of Jefferies' continued rebuilding and he left the club towards the end of the following season on a free transfer to St Johnstone. Having scored 101 goals in his two periods at the club, Colquhoun was the last Hearts player to score a century of goals for the club.

He decided to hang up his boots at the age of 34 to pursue a career as a media pundit.

Born: Stirling, July 14, 1963.
Signed from: Celtic.
Debut: August 10, 1985, Premier League Hearts 1 Celtic 1.
Appearances: 496. Goals: 101.
International honours: Scotland (1).

BARNEY BATTLES

 arney Battles possesses a record that he is unlikely to relinquish. If Bauld, Conn, Wardhaugh and Robertson all managed more goals in maroon, then it was only because they played more matches for the club.

In season 1930-31, the towering striker scored a remarkable 44 league goals for the club - a record that stands firmly intact to this day. Given that those 44 goals came in just 35 matches, then it is a mark of how accomplished a chance-taker he was. In all, he averaged more than a goal a game for the club by scoring 218 times in 200 first-team appearances.

Battles senior died shortly before his son was born and as a teenager, the younger Battles emigrated to America with his mother. But he had developed a love of football from an early age and even in America, where it was less fashionable, he managed to find his way to a professional club.

The first American professional league had been established in 1921 and Battles junior signed for Boston AL as their first professional in 1926.

He impressed to such an extent that he went on to represent the United States in a match against Canada in Montreal on June 27, 1925, which the Americans lost 1-0. It was to be his only international cap for his adopted country but two of his team-mates that day, goalkeeper James Douglas and forward Thomas Florie, went on to play for the USA in the first World Cup in Uruguay five years later.

Battles returned to Scotland in 1928 and Hearts beat Rangers and Celtic to the player's signature. The new recruit was reportedly given a £20 signing-on fee and paid £9 a week. A crowd of 18,000 turned up to witness his first match - a trial game amongst Hearts players - and he scored four times. It was a taste of what was to come from the powerful striker.

He scored on his league debut against Queen's Park at Hampden and he hit his first hat-trick soon afterwards in a game against Hamilton at Tynecastle. He went one better in September, 1928, when he found the net four times in a 7-3 win over Ayr United. There was understandable interest from top English clubs at the time, with Arsenal reported to be one of them and he went on to score 31 league goals during his first season at Tynecastle.

He also scored 11 goals in three successive matches against Hibernian in 1929 - in the Dunedin Cup, the Wilson Cup and the Charity Cup. Not only was he such a talent with either foot but he was a menace to opposing defenders with his ability in the air. If ever there was a natural goalscorer, then it was Battles.

He had scored 100 goals in 93 appearances and his 44-goal tally in the league of 1930-31 would surely have been further improved upon if he had not missed several matches due to a bout of appendicitis.

Remarkably, Battles was to win only one full international cap for Scotland - against Wales in a 1-1 draw at Hampden in 1931 - although he was a regular pick with the Scottish League team.

He had a cartilage operation in the autumn of that year, which kept him out of the first-team for five months and he broke down again not long after his return. Battles was to retire prematurely from the game in 1936 at the age of 30. But his records linger on and his scoring exploits in the 1930-31 season are virtually set in stone.

Born: Fisherrow, October, 1905.
Signed from: Boston AL.
Debut: August, 1928, First Division: Queen's Park v Hearts.
Appearances: 200. Goals: 218.
International honours: USA (1), Scotland (1).

GILLES ROUSSET

Jim Jefferies had been in the manager's chair at Tynecastle less than three months when he chose to try out his fourth goalkeeper of the season. Henry Smith, Craig Nelson and Gary O'Connor had all been given chances but when the manager saw the chance to get a goalkeeper who had an international pedigree, he did not hesitate.

Gilles Rousset arrived at Tynecastle with an impressive track record, having played twice for the French national team and played club football with Lyon, Marseilles, Sochaux and Rennes. He was the first of the foreign imports to arrive but a considerable number were to follow, as Jefferies used the Bosman ruling to advantage.

The 6'5" goalkeeper made his debut in a 2-0 defeat by Falkirk at Brockville in October, 1995. It was a result that left Hearts bottom of the Premier League and it made it clear to Jefferies that more surgery was required. The goalkeeper had, nonetheless, made a respectable debut and he kept clean sheets in his next two matches to steady the ship.

An imposing goalkeeper who commands his area, Rousset stands up well to opposing forwards and is remarkably agile. A great shot-stopper, he is also good on the ground as he can get down low to shots - not easy for such a towering figure.

An important player for Hearts during their run to the Scottish Cup Final in his first season and if he dropped a clanger for Rangers' second goal from Brian Laudrup in the 5-1 defeat, then it was totally out of character. Indeed, in the six games he played leading up to the final, he had only lost three goals and it had helped Hearts to fourth place in the league after their poor start.

Rousset showed that he had not let the error in the cup final upset him, when he made a good start to the following season - an unblemished match in a goalless draw with Red Star Belgrade away from home and his consistency helped Hearts into the final of the League Cup. But it was the genius of Paul Gascoigne that inspired Rangers to another victory that day.

A measure of his consistency could be seen in the fact that he only lost eight goals in his final 12 matches for Hearts in the 1996-97 season and he had established himself as the undisputed number one at Tynecastle.

Rousset also had a big part to play the following season, as Hearts pushed hard for silverware in the league and the Scottish Cup and if the team was to fall short of glory in the league, then Rousset crowned his season with a magnificent performance in the cup final.

He was rightly voted "Man of the Match", as he chased away the demons of the 1996 final and produced a string of superb saves to ensure that Hearts finally won some silverware.

Rousset had another consistent season in 1998-99 and if it was a struggle for Hearts to match their form of the previous year, the goalkeeper stood tall to help his team finish the season strongly.

Born: Hyeres, France, August 22, 1963.
Signed from: Rennes (France).
Debut: October 28, 1995, Premier Division, Falkirk 2 Hearts 0.
Appearances: 158.
International honours: France (2).

JIM CRUICKSHANK

im Cruickshank spent 17 years keeping goal for Hearts between 1960-77, yet for all his considerable endeavours, he ended his career at Tynecastle with no club honours.

He was to play in all 34 of Hearts' league matches in the 1964-65 season, when the team was just a goal shy of winning the title and he also played in the 1968 Scottish Cup Final against Dunfermline and the 1976 final, when Rangers beat Hearts 3-1. He played in the League Cup Final replay in 1961, deputising for Gordon Marshall but was again on the losing side against Rangers.

There was consolation for Cruickshank in the shape of half a dozen international caps for Scotland but regarded by many as Hearts' finest goalkeeper, it was ironic that he had nothing tangible to show for his long years at the club.

Yet there were plenty of memories, not least of which was a triple penalty save from Joe Davis in an Edinburgh derby in 1967.

An agile and reliable goalkeeper, Cruickshank was noted for his consistency and he went on to play over 600 games for the club, almost 400 of which were in the league.

He stood only 5'10" but his athleticism - he was a Scottish schoolboys' long-jump champion - made up for his lack of inches and he proved a formidable barrier to opposing forwards. Not only was he confident of taking crosses but he had the ability to pull off spectacular saves.

Cruickshank signed for Hearts from his first senior club, Queen's Park, in May, 1960 and by the age of 17, had played for the first-team. Capped at Schoolboy, Youth, Under-23, Amateur and Scottish League level, he won his first full cap in 1964 against West Germany. It was to be another six years before he was capped again - against Wales - and his Scotland career was to span 12 years, as his final international appearance was against Romania in 1976.

The Glasgow-born goalkeeper made his debut in October, 1960, at Somerset Park, when Hearts went down narrowly, 1-0, to Ayr United and although he went on to play four more times that season (including his first clean sheet in a 9-0 cup win over Tarff Rovers), it was not until the start of the 1963-64 season that he became a regular first-choice.

In fact, he did not miss a league match for four years, by which time Kenny Garland was challenging him for his place; but Cruickshank was to hold his colleague at bay and when he left the club in 1977, Garland had already given up the game, frustrated at his lack of opportunities.

Cruickshank had a remarkable 102 clean sheets in 394 league appearances, which was a healthy number, given that Hearts did not enjoy the best of times during that period.

Born: Glasgow, April 13, 1941.
Signed from: Queen's Park.
Debut: October 15, 1960, First Division, Ayr United 1 Hearts 0.
Appearances: 610.
International honours: Scotland (6).

WALTER KIDD

If ever there was a player who gave everything for Hearts, it was Walter Kidd. He epitomised the Alex MacDonald era, as he was able and industrious and always willing to run that extra yard to help out a colleague.

He was to play over 500 games for the club, many as captain and the fact that he did not become the first Hearts captain to touch silverware in a generation was as much down to bad luck as anything else, particularly when the team went so close in 1986.

Signed from Newtongrange Star in 1977 after Celtic had allowed him to move on, Kidd started out in midfield and made his debut in the First Division when he came on as a substitute at Links Park in a 3-1 defeat by Montrose in October, 1977. It was a team that included the likes of Jim Jefferies, Eamonn Bannon, Drew Busby and Donald Park.

Throughout his career, Kidd was not noted for his goalscoring exploits but his first for the club proved invaluable, as it came in the second leg of the League Cup quarter final with Dundee United the following month. Hearts trailed 3-1 from the first leg but with 19 year-old Kidd scoring the opener early in the second half, Hearts clawed it back to 3-3 on aggregate in the return at Tynecastle.

Kidd and Hearts achieved promotion at the end of the season, although there were no further goals from the youngster, who had now taken over from Jim Brown at right-back.

With that final promotion in 1983 under Alex MacDonald, there emerged a new and more resilient Hearts. Kidd had managed his first Premier League goal in a 1-1 draw with Partick Thistle in February, 1981 and his next did not come until three years later, this time in a 3-1 defeat by Dundee United at Tannadice.

The 1985-86 season was to prove an eventful one for Hearts and Kidd. The captain was sent off along with team-mate, Sandy Clark and Rangers' Ally McCoist in an early-season match at Ibrox, which Hearts lost 3-1.

As Hearts went so close to the title, only to be pipped on the final day by Celtic, so the frustration was obvious in the Scottish Cup Final against Alex Ferguson's Aberdeen at Hampden. Kidd summed it up when he was sent off near the end of the final - which Hearts lost 3-0 - after throwing the ball at Frank McDougall, the Aberdeen striker. He had earlier been booked and Kidd later admitted it was a moment of madness that had left referee Hugh Alexander no option but to send him off - the first cup final captain to receive his marching orders.

Kidd was to give Hearts great service for a few more seasons and was still as dependable as ever as the team pushed, unsuccessfully, for honours. His final start was Alex MacDonald's last game in charge - a 3-1 defeat by Rangers at Tynecastle and although he played five more matches as a substitute, it was clear that he was not part of new manager, Joe Jordan's plans.

After 14 years at Tynecastle, he was released but his career was not over. After joining Aidrie, he was part of the team that reached the 1992 Scottish Cup Final (beating Hearts on penalty kicks in the semi final) but went down 2-1 to Rangers.

Kidd has since moved into coaching and after spending time at Falkirk, he is, at the time of writing, assisting former Tynecastle team-mate, Gary Mackay at Airdrie.

Born: Edinburgh, March 10, 1958.
Signed from: Newtongrange Star.
Debut: October 19, 1977, First Division, Montrose 3 Hearts 1.
Appearances: 544. Goals: 15.
International honours: 0.

PERCY DAWSON

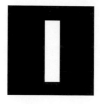f Barney Battles is to go down in history as the most prolific of Hearts' goalscorers, given the return he gave for the number of matches he played, Percy Dawson is not far behind.

This powerfully-built centre-forward scored 99 goals in just 117 competitive matches for Hearts after he came north in early 1911 from North Shields Athletic for a modest sum of £100.

Brought up in the north-east of England, it did not take him long to settle at Tynecastle and with the help of Bobby Walker, he went on to become Hearts' top scorer for three successive seasons, 1911-12, 1912-13 and 1913-14.

A player of considerable pace and ability, who could score from any distance, he was soon attracting the interest of the top English clubs.

Dawson was one of the key players in what was widely regarded as one of the best teams in Hearts' history, with the likes of Walker, Bob Mercer and Paddy Crossan all in their ranks - a side compiled at a total cost of just £15,000.

Hearts lost 1-0 in the Scottish Cup semi final to Falkirk in 1913 and the following season, with Dawson again prominent, they looked capable of winning the league; but the loss of their star centre-forward in the February did not help their cause and they eventually finished third behind champions, Celtic and runners-up, Rangers.

Hearts had been keen to hold onto Dawson but were also in the process of rebuilding their ground and as the costs of constructing the present main stand went beyond the estimates, it left the club in a dilemma.

As it turned out, Dawson had to be sacrificed to allow the club to pay for the stand and Blackburn Rovers were more than happy to pay a then British record transfer fee of £2,500 for his considerable talents.

Dawson - who scored 64 goals in his 80 league matches for Hearts - was to spend ten years at Blackburn and won a League Championship medal within a few months of joining them, in what was to be their last English title until Kenny Dalglish steered them to the Championship again in 1995.

Born: North Shields, 1890.
Signed from: North Shields Athletic.
Debut: January 14, 1911, First Division: Partick Thistle v Hearts.
Appearances: 117. Goals: 99.
International honours: 0.

JOHNNY HAMILTON

Johnny Hamilton was one of the big personality players at Tynecastle in the late fifties and early sixties. The diminutive winger, brought up in Lanarkshire, was one of the 'tanner ba' players whose demise is sorely missed in the Scottish game and his dribbling skills were a feature of the team that had a hat-trick of League Cup successes between 1958-62, scoring in two finals.

Signed in April, 1955, Hamilton made his debut in October that year in a 4-1 win at Airdrie in the league. His first goal had arrived - conveniently enough - shortly before Christmas, in a 7-1 destruction of Motherwell at Tynecastle, on a day when Jimmy Wardhaugh scored four and Willie Bauld the other two.

Hamilton was more of a provider than a goalscorer and his pace and close-control created many chances for the more natural scorers around him. He played only four matches in the Championship-winning season of 1957-58 (and remarkably, also scored four times!) but he was more established in the team when Hearts won the title again in 1960, playing 27 matches and contributing seven goals.

He was on target in two successive League Cup Finals, scoring once in the 5-1 final win over Partick Thistle at Hampden in 1958 and the equaliser, with a 30-yard shot, in the 2-1 win over Third Lanark the following year.

Hamilton had established himself as a regular first-choice player and his crowd-pleasing skills made him a huge favourite with the supporters. He was also a reliable penalty taker and scored 20 goals from the spot in his time at Tynecastle.

By the early sixties, he was beginning to make more of a mark in front of goal. He scored 20 times in all competitions in 1963-64 to finish third-top scorer behind Willie Wallace and Tommy White and then 21 the following season to finish behind Wallace and Alan Gordon.

Hamilton also has the distinction of being Hearts' first-ever substitute. On August 20, 1966, he replaced Chris Shevlane in a 4-3 win over Clyde in the League Cup, an occasion also notable for the fact that Willie Wallace scored all four of Hearts' goals.

Hamilton went on to score 157 goals (including 20 penalties) for Hearts before leaving to join Watford in 1967. Full international honours eluded Hamilton at a time when there were so many great Scottish wingers but he was capped at Under-23 level and earned a Scottish League call-up in 1958.

Born: Larkhall, January 22, 1935.
Signed from: Lesmahagow Juniors.
Debut: October 1, 1955, First Division, Airdrie 1 Hearts 4.
Appearances: 496. Goals: 157.
International honours: 0.

COLIN CAMERON

t may seem premature to include Colin Cameron in such a collection of Hearts greats this early in his Tynecastle career but in the short time he has worn maroon, his influence has been significant.

Cameron, born in Kirkcaldy, started his career at Raith Rovers and after being farmed out to Sligo Rovers to complete his apprenticeship, he returned to help Jimmy Nicholl's side win two First Division titles, in 1993 and 1995 and most notably, the League Cup, after a thrilling penalty shoot-out with Celtic at Ibrox in 1994.

An industrious and intelligent midfield player, his ability to arrive late in the penalty area is a hallmark of his game and he is a player who earned rave reviews during his time at Raith.

Standing only 5'6", Cameron gained a reputation as one of the fittest players in the Scottish game, as he motored between penalty boxes, helping out both his defence and his attack.

He had also gained some European experience with Raith as they had qualified for the UEFA Cup and played in two matches against Bayern Munich.

Several clubs took notice and there was genuine interest from Aberdeen but Jim Jefferies moved swiftly to bring him to Hearts in 1996, just before the transfer deadline, in a £400,000 deal that took John Millar to Raith in part-exchange.

He had an immediate impact in his first game, as Hearts beat Rangers 2-0 and three days later, Cameron was back at Stark's Park and scored for Hearts in a 3-1 win. Rather bizarrely, he also collected a trophy that day, as Raith supporters had voted him their 'Player of the Year' but could not have anticipated that they would be presenting their award to a Hearts player!

Cameron scored again - against Motherwell in a 1-1 draw - before the end of the season but it was just to provide Hearts with a taster of what was to follow. He missed the Scottish Cup Final against Rangers as he was cup-tied and so had not played in a losing Hearts team since he signed.

Indeed, that sequence was extended at the start of the following season and included two European Cup-Winners' Cup matches against Red Star Belgrade, although Hearts went out on the 'away-goals' rule.

But there was a 4-0 defeat at Aberdeen to bring him back down to earth. There was soon to be some success, however, as Hearts progressed to the final of the League Cup and Cameron scored in two of the ties en route - at St Johnstone and against Dundee in the semi final at Easter Road.

Unfortunately, there was not to be another winner's medal for Cameron, as Hearts lost narrowly, 4-3, to Rangers in the final. The midfield player did not miss a match for Hearts that season and indeed had the distinction of being the only player of any Premier Division side to play every match for his club.

Cameron was also proving accurate from the penalty spot and thus adding to his goal tally. He kept his nerve admirably to score a last-minute penalty winner against St Johnstone in November, 1997, as Hearts embarked on a tremendous run that took them to the top of the Premier Division.

It was a season in which Hearts kept apace with Rangers and Celtic thanks to great consistency against the other clubs in the division. But Cameron had picked up a stomach injury towards the end of the campaign, which threatened to keep him out of the Scottish Cup Final against Rangers.

Fortunately for Hearts' supporters, he was passed fit to play and his nerve was tested again when Hearts won a penalty within 90 seconds of kick-off. Cameron admitted he changed his mind about which way to place his kick during the run-up but whatever his thoughts, he steered the ball well clear of Andy Goram to give Hearts the lead.

It was the goal that set Hearts on the way to their first silverware for 36 years.

However, in 1998-99, Cameron sat out most of the campaign through injury and manager, Jim Jefferies, admitted he was the one player his team sorely missed, as they slumped to the bottom of the new Scottish Premier League.

However, his return coincided with Hearts' return to form. He scored a memorable goal in a win at Dundee United and then, more crucially, twice in the win over Dunfermline at Tynecastle that ensured Hearts' safety.

Rather remarkably, given that he had missed such a huge chunk of the season, he was called up by Craig Brown for international duty and made his debut in the friendly win over Germany in 1999.

His importance to Hearts was acknowledged by Jefferies at the start of the 1999-2000 season, when he appointed his midfield player club captain.

Born: Kirkcaldy, October 23, 1972.
Signed from: Raith Rovers.
Debut: April 10, 1996, Premier Division, Hearts 2 Rangers 0.
Appearances: 107. Goals: 30.
International honours: Scotland (2).

JACK HARKNESS

Like another great Hearts goalkeeper, Jim Cruickshank, Jack Harkness started out on his senior career with amateur side, Queen's Park. Like Cruickshank some 30 years later, he was destined to stand between the posts at Tynecastle during a time when no trophies were won.

Born in Glasgow in 1907, he went on to play for Scotland at schoolboy, amateur and full international level before he was 20.

An agile and capable goalkeeper who had a reputation for fair play, Harkness went on to play twelve times for his country, nine of which were during his time at Tynecastle. To this day, he is still Hearts' most-capped goalkeeper.

Harkness signed for Hearts in May, 1928 and went on to play over 400 matches for the club in a period spanning eight years.

He built up a reputation for being a solid and at times, courageous goalkeeper and famously, was a member of the 'Wembley Wizards' team that crushed England 5-1 in 1928.

Harkness was capped against England four times, against Wales four times, against Ireland on three occasions and once, in 1932, against France.

Unfortunately, a bad leg injury meant that the goalkeeper had to retire from the game prematurely at the age of 30 and Huddersfield Town provided the opposition for his benefit match in 1934.

Harkness kept a clean sheet in that match in a 3-0 win and only Henry Smith and Jim Cruickshank have gone on to record more shut-outs as Hearts goalkeepers, with Harkness totting up 34.

After hanging up his gloves, Harkness went on to write about the game and was one of the most respected sports journalists of his generation.

Born: Glasgow, 1907.
Signed from: Queen's Park.
Appearances: 400.

CRAIG LEVEIN

Craig Levein was one of the most accomplished central defenders of his generation.

It was obvious, even from his teenage years, when he made his senior debut for Cowdenbeath in a goalless draw against Brechin City, that he was destined to make a name for himself in the game.

Several Premier Division clubs watched him in those early days but it was the lottery of a cup draw that was to eventually take him to Tynecastle. Cowdenbeath were drawn against Hearts in the League Cup at the start of the 1983-84 season and Levein's performance in the two matches impressed then manager, Alex MacDonald. A sum of just £35,000 was enough to persuade Cowdenbeath to part with their most-prized asset in November, 1983.

Less than a month later, the central defender (originally signed by Pat Stanton at Cowdenbeath) was making his league debut for Hearts at Ibrox as a 19 year-old.

It did not take Levein long to establish a regular place in the team and he was to go on and play over 450 first-team games for the club, including friendlies.

He scored a total of 21 goals for Hearts - his first competitive one coming in a 4-0 League Cup win over East Stirling in November, 1984.

Unfortunately, Levein's career was blighted by two serious knee injuries and he was forced to prematurely retire from the game in his early thirties to pursue a career in coaching and management.

His first setback came in a reserve fixture against Hibernian at Easter Road, when he caught his studs in the turf and twisted his knee. After seeing a specialist shortly afterwards, he was told to consider hanging up his boots but after seeking a second opinion, he was informed that the cruciate ligament damage could be repaired.

Levein was out for 11 months but came back stronger than ever. In January, 1988, his knee gave way again during a match against Rangers at Tynecastle and he was out for another year. Again, he came back courageously and it was his feeling that, having lost a chunk of his career through injury, it would give him a chance to continue for longer at the end of it. It was not to be.

However, to dwell on the injuries does Levein a disservice. If he was robbed of a chance to play for longer and be part of the Hearts team that was eventually to end their long spell without silverware in 1998, he will always be remembered as a gifted, athletic defender who could shine in the best of international company.

He missed the league title decider with Dundee in 1986 after suffering a virus on the eve of the match and many believe that, had Levein been fit to take his place in central defence at Dens Park that day, Hearts would not have leaked the late goals that so cruelly cost them a Championship.

Levein, born in Dunfermline, went on to make 16 full international appearances for Scotland after making his debut in a 1-0 win over Argentina in March, 1990.

He played with distinction in the 2-1 win over Sweden at the 1990 World Cup in Italy but a thigh injury sustained in that match meant he missed the final group match against Brazil.

He captained Scotland in a friendly international against Germany at Ibrox in 1993, becoming the first Hearts player to captain Scotland since Dave Mackay in 1958.

Levein's final appearance for his country was in the 1-1 draw with Russia at Hampden in a European Championship qualifying match but he would surely have won many more international caps had he not been cut down by injuries.

He played under managers such as Alex Ferguson, Andy Roxburgh, Alex MacDonald and Jim Jefferies and now wants to cut his own niche as a manager.

After a short spell as coach with Livingston, Levein accepted an offer to go back to his roots and take over as manager of Cowdenbeath. It is there, as in his playing days, that he would serve his apprenticeship.

Born: Dunfermline, October 22, 1964.
Signed from: Cowdenbeath.
Debut: December 3, 1983, Premier League, Rangers 3 Hearts 0.
Appearances: 462. Goals: 21.
International honours: Scotland (16).

BOBBY KIRK

obby Kirk was a model of consistency for Hearts throughout their most successfull spell. The rugged full-back filled the shirt vacated by Bobby Parker and went on to help Hearts to the Scottish Cup of 1956 in his first season and become a stalwart of the League Championship-winning teams of 1958 and 1960. There were also League Cup winners' medals in 1958 and 1959 and a runners-up medal in the 1961 competition, when Hearts lost in the final to Rangers.

Kirk was a Scotland junior cap with Arniston Rangers and was signed up by Dunfermline in 1947. At East End Park, he helped Dunfermline to the 1949 League Cup Final, where they went down 3-0 to East Fife. He was transferred to Raith Rovers in 1953 and Hearts took him to Tynecastle two years later, when they paid out £2,500 for his services.

Kirk was to become a mainstay as Hearts enjoyed the best spell in their history and from November 30, 1957, until October 8, 1960, he only missed one match for the club. He was also an expert at penalty kicks and scored 12 goals from the spot - a one hundred per cent record - during his time at Tynecastle. These were the only goals he scored for Hearts.

His main assets were his defensive qualities and his ability to read the game and cover for his team-mates was a facet of his play. Kirk also gained plenty of European experience, as Hearts entered this arena for the first time against Standard Liege in 1958 and he also played in ties against Benfica and Inter Milan in later years.

He was unfortunate not to win a full international cap at any stage, although he did gain a Scotland 'B' cap against England in 1956-57.

Kirk retired from the game in April, 1963 after playing over 350 matches for the club. He spent some time as manager of Gala Fairydean and went on to work with the 'Hearts Colts' from 1967-71.

Born: Arniston, August 12, 1927.
Signed from: Raith Rovers.
Debut: August 13, 1955, League Cup, Partick Thistle 0 Hearts 2.
Appearances: 365. Goals: 12.
International honours: 0.

JIMMY MURRAY

Jimmy Murray was a key figure for Hearts when they finally won the League Championship in 1958 - the first time in 61 years. A livewire forward, he netted an astonishing 27 goals in 33 league matches, as Hearts took the title with a record goals tally.

Born in Edinburgh, Murray showed promise from an early age and was capped by Scotland at schoolboy level. A regular goalscorer, he joined Hearts from Merchiston Thistle in September, 1950 and made his debut against Stirling Albion in March, 1952, when he scored in a 5-2 win as he deputised for Willie Bauld. It was his one and only game that season but he had given an early indication of his instinct for goal.

He spent most of his early years at Tynecstle in the reserves before he was called up for national service with the RAF, where he played representative football and also played as a guest for Reading.

He was back in the Hearts team in 1955, when he played four games in April at the end of a season in which Hearts had won the League Cup and were to finish fourth in the league, ten points behind champions, Aberdeen. Murray filled in for Alfie Conn on three occasions and then Bauld again but this time there were no goals to savour.

In Hearts' Championship-winning season, Murray and Young hit 51 league goals between them, with the latter managing a healthy return of 24 in 34 matches. If Murray's goal return was remarkable, then he was - to an extent - overshadowed by Jimmy Wardhaugh, who scored 28 in 30 league games and was overall top scorer that season, with 37 goals.

But from mid-December to the end of March, Murray scored 17 goals in 15 matches in the league, including a hat-trick in a 4-0 win over Airdrie and he also scored in Scottish Cup ties against East Fife and Hibernian.

A robust centre-forward who was always on the look-out for scraps in and around the penalty area, Murray worked hard for his chances and to cap his memorable season, he was called up to Scotland's World Cup squad for Sweden.

He earned the distinction of being the first Scotsman to score a goal in the final stages of the World Cup. Scotland had qualified for the finals in 1954 but had not managed a single goal until Murray finally broke the deadlock in Scotland's opening match against Yugoslavia in Vasteras in a 1-1 draw. Ironically, Wardaugh did not make the final 22 after being named in Scotland's original squad of 40.

Murray went on to play against France in the World Cup in Sweden and won a total of five international caps after making an impressive debut against England in a 1-1 draw at Hampden.

Murray's scoring streak continued in 1958-59, when he scored 19 goals in all competitions, including a double in the 5-1 League Cup Final win over Partick Thistle at Hampden, which earned him another medal. Hearts finished two points behind Rangers in the Championship race but Murray contributed a valuable 11 goals in 18 league matches the following season, as Hearts regained the title.

He left Hearts in 1961 after 63 league goals for the club and joined Falkirk, for whom he continued to bang in the goals.

Born: Edinburgh, February 4, 1933.
Signed from: Merchiston Thistle.
Debut: March 15, 1952, First Division, Hearts 5 Stirling Albion 2.
Appearances: 191. Goals: 103.
International honours: Scotland (5).

WILLIE HAMILTON

Born in Chapelhall, Willie Hamilton started his career with Sheffield United, where he spent six years before joining Middlesbrough. The talented inside-left joined Hearts in June, 1962, at the age of 25, when he was signed from the Ayresome Park club for a £2,500 fee.

He joined Hearts at a time when they were undergoing a significant change in personnel after finishing sixth the previous season and runners-up in the League Cup to Rangers. Willie Bauld had left the club at the end of that season following his retirement after 16 years at the club and the popular Bobby Blackwood had been sold to Ipswich for £10,000.

Hamilton immediately struck up a rapport with the Tynecastle faithful, with his astute play and vision on the ball. He made a scoring debut in a vital 2-0 League Cup qualifying group win over Dundee at Tynecastle - a result that meant Hearts qualified for the last eight ahead of Celtic.

It was to prove significant, as Hearts went on to dismiss Morton (6-1 on aggregate) in the quarter final, when Hamilton was also on the mark in the return leg and Second Division St Johnstone, 4-0 in the semi final at Easter Road, when the inside forward dominated the proceedings and scored one of the goals himself.

Kilmarnock awaited in the final at Hampden and it was Hamilton who created what proved to be the winning goal, when he raced down the left wing and cut the ball back for Norrie Davidson to net. It was Hearts' first trophy for two-and-a-half years but few could have expected that it would be their last for almost 36 years.

Hamilton was to score a respectable 13 goals in 33 matches that season, as Hearts went on to finish fifth in the league. But his career at Tynecastle was to be short-lived and he was to fall foul of the club's strict disciplinary code.

He played only four matches for Hearts in the 1963-64 campaign and his last game for the club was at the end of October, in 1963, when he scored in a 3-1 defeat by Kilmarnock at Rugby Park.

Hamilton was transferred to Hibernian for just £6,000. He was capped by the Scottish League against the Italian League while at Tynecastle but his only full cap - against Finland in 1965 - came when he was at Easter Road.

Hamilton later joined Aston Villa before returning to Tynecastle in 1967, much to the delight of the supporters. Although he was not as sharp as in his previous spell, he played another 33 matches for the club and scored seven goals.

He played for a spell in South Africa after leaving Tynecastle and then emigrated to Canada, where he died at the age of just 37.

Hearts historian, Bill Smith, assesses: "Willie Hamilton was the most complete footballer I have ever seen. He was equally good with his right foot and his left foot and he was simply a wizard with a football."

Born: Chapelhall, February 16, 1938.
Signed from: Middlesbrough.
Debut: September 1, 1962, League Cup, Hearts 2 Dundee 0.
Appearances: 74. Goals: 24.
International honours: Scotland (1).

PADDY CROSSAN

addy Crossan was one of the most popular defenders to wear maroon. The uncompromising full-back gave the club 14 years' service between 1911-25, after signing from junior side, Arniston Rangers.

Strong in the tackle and a towering presence in the Hearts defence, he was converted from a half-back to playing a deeper role. His talents brought him to the fringes of the Scotland international team but he did not manage a full cap, although played for the Scottish League against the Southern League in 1914.

Crossan was one of the 16 Hearts players who volunteered to fight in the First World War. He was wounded in the Battle of the Somme in 1916 and later gassed while on active service.

Nevertheless, he came back to play for Hearts for another seven years after the end of the war, when he was first-choice in his position. Such was his popularity at the time, he was given two benefit matches by the club - against a Scotland Select in 1920 and against Manchester United four years later. He was eventually given a free transfer and signed for Leith Athletic in 1925.

He opened a public house in Edinburgh's Rose Street when he retired from the game but he died in April, 1933 at the young age of 39 - his early death brought on by his wartime experiences.

An obituary notice at the time declared that he was more 'personality' than player but paid further tribute by stating that he was "perhaps the most whole hearted player that ever wore the maroon jersey. He would never accept defeat until the final whistle went and his cheery disposition was always an inspiration to his team-mates to stick in. He had the happy knack of coming up smiling when things went against him."

Born: Addiewell, 1893.
Signed from: Arniston Rangers.
Appearances: 380.
International honours: 0.

DAVIE HOLT

**D**ependable Davie Holt was almost a permanent fixture at left-back for Hearts between 1961-67. Strong in the tackle and a player with supreme fitness, few wingers enjoyed playing against him.

He was a late starter to the professional game after playing amateur for several seasons and he even had a spell at Stockton Amateurs when he was in the RAF. He joined Queen's Park in 1957 at the age of 21 and he played for Scotland at Under-23 level and Great Britain at the 1960 Olympic Games in Rome.

Holt turned professional when he joined Hearts in September, 1960, at the age of 24 and made his debut in a 2-2 draw with Airdrie at Broomfield that month. He went on to play 24 games for Hearts that season, as the team finished mid-table but he was fighting for the left-back berth with George Thomson and Danny Ferguson.

By the start of the 1961-62 season, he was first choice and played in the two League Cup Final matches with Rangers, a 1-1 draw and a 3-1 replay defeat. Indeed, Holt was the only player who played in all 51 matches for Hearts that season and if goals were not part of his repertoire (he did not score a single competitive goal in his time at Tynecastle), then he was no less thought of.

He won a League Cup winners' medal in 1962, when Hearts beat Kilmarnock 1-0 in the Final at Hampden and went on to play 350 games for the club. He rarely ventured across his own halfway line but such was his consistency that he was called up for international duty.

However, his Scotland debut against Austria at Hampden in 1963 was marred by controversy. With Scotland leading 4-1, the match had to be abandonded after 79 minutes due to the rough play of the Austrians. Holt went on to win five full caps for his country, also playing against Norway, the Republic of Ireland, Spain and West Germany and surely would have won more but for having the misfortune to be competing with Rangers' Eric Caldow for an international berth.

By the late sixties, Holt was competing for his first-team place with the emerging Arthur Mann. In 1967-68, Mann took over from the more experienced player halfway through the season and although Holt played three matches in April when Mann was injured, it was the younger player who was given the nod for the Scottish Cup Final against Dunfermline at the end of that month.

Holt was given a recall the following December after Mann had been signed by Manchester City for £65,000 and he went on to play 26 games that season. He played his last game for the club in April, 1969 - a 2-2 draw with Arbroath - and teenager, Billy McAlpine, took his place briefly the following season before giving way to Peter Oliver.

Holt left Hearts at the age of 33 and went on to join Partick Thistle.

Born: Glasgow, January 3, 1936.
Signed from: Queen's Park.
Debut: September 24, 1960, Airdrie 2 Hearts 2.
Appearances: 350. Goals: 0.
International honours: Scotland (5).

DONALD FORD

Hearts found a natural successor to Willie Wallace - who had departed for Celtic - in Donald Ford. The slightly-built centre-forward was top scorer for the club through eight successive seasons between 1968-75 and his goalscoring feats were to take him all the way to the World Cup finals in Germany in 1974.

Ford, who was also an accomplished cricketer, although a full international cap at that sport eluded him, played as an amateur at Hearts between 1964-67, as he was studying to become a chartered accountant.

He made his debut as a 19 year-old in a 4-2 win over Celtic in September, 1964 and went on to make nine appearances that first season, scoring three goals. However, he had to watch from the stands in disbelief when Kilmarnock somehow wrestled the title away from Tynecastle on the final day of that season.

There was little consolation for the team when they beat Kilmarnock 8-3 in an experimental match without 'offside' shortly afterwards but Ford scored five goals that day and it remains one of his career highlights.

However, it was not until the departure of Wallace that he started to make a significant impact. In 1967-68, Ford scored 16 goals, including a Scottish Cup quarter-final replay winner against Rangers at Tynecastle, which he still remembers fondly. Hearts reached the Scottish Cup Final that year but lost 3-1 to Dunfermline and while Ford acknowledges the disappointment, he believes the better team won on the day.

"Dunfermline deserved to win. Man-for-man, they were the better team and they had a terrific blend of enthusiasm, strength and skill. Alex Edwards was a big factor and I think they were also better prepared for the final," he concedes.

"The highlights for me were scoring the five goals against Kilmarnock in that 'offside' trial match. Scoring the winner in the Scottish Cup quarter-final replay against Rangers in 1968 was also a highlight, as was when I scored a hat-trick in a 4-1 win over Partick Thistle in the Scottish Cup in 1974. Willie Ormond, then the Scotland manager, was watching the game and it was one of my best for Hearts and I'm sure it was a big factor in my call-up for the international team," he assesses.

"I also enjoyed playing in the Texaco Cup competition in the early seventies. We had two great semi-final matches with Motherwell in 1971 when we reached the final and I also remember we had two terrific games with Burnley that season.

"They had a very strong side and included Ralph Coates - soon to join Spurs. They cuffed us down there and should have won by six or seven but in the end it was only 3-1 and we won the return 4-1 at Tynecastle to go through."

During November, 1971, Ford hit a rich seam of goals and scored two hat-tricks in three matches - scoring three times in a 6-1 win over Morton and then another three in a 3-2 win over Aberdeen. Sandwiched between the games, Ford also hit the only goal in a win over Ayr United. Ford also achieved the rare distinction of scoring a hat-trick of penalties - in a 3-2 win over Morton in 1973.

It was during that 1973-74 season that Hearts played what Ford believes was some of their best football for years and they led the league after the first couple of months.

"We had a great team that year, with the likes of Kenny Aird, Rab Prentice and Drew Busby and we played entertaining football, with two wingers. Busby was knocking the ball down for me and I went on to score 29 goals that season," he recalls.

"But we just didn't have the depth of squad to sustain it. Once injuries and suspensions caught up with us, we were struggling to keep it going. I think if we had three or four more quality players to come in, we would have won the league that season."

Ford played under a number of managers at Tynecastle and was signed by the great Tommy Walker. "Tommy Walker was not someone I knew very well, as he was the old secretary-manager type and the players wouldn't see him during the week," he explains.

"It was John Harvey who took training and he was the most fantastic trainer and worked really well with the players. But I don't think he was manager material and when he was promoted upstairs, it didn't really work out. I also had a great respect for Jock Wallace, who took over as trainer.

"But it was a difficult time for the club after a period when they had enjoyed so much success and really Hearts just drifted along in those years.

"Jim Jefferies was breaking into the team just before I left and it's funny but at the time, he was not someone who I said would have been the type to go into management. But then it's difficult as a player to look around the dressing-room and pick out who would make a good manager. Who would have said, when he was a player, that someone like Alex Ferguson would become one of the best managers in the game?"

Ford went on to make his international debut against Czechoslovakia in a World Cup qualifier in Ocotber, 1973, in Prague and earned two further caps against West Germany and Wales. He travelled to the World Cup finals in Germany in 1974 but did not play in any of the three matches.

"I count myself fortunate to have gone to the World Cup. I didn't consider myself an international player and at Hearts, I had to always work at my game. I had an eye for goal and was quick but Joe Harper was a much better player than me and he would have gone to Germany but for an injury. Dixie Deans was also ahead of me but I think he was also injured and couldn't go. But it was a great privilege to be there as there, were so many great players in that team and we came within a centimetre of qualifying for the next stage," he says candidly.

Ford scored a total of 188 goals in 436 matches for Hearts and left in May, 1976, for a spell at Falkirk. He went on to work as a radio commentator and being a keen photographer, he now presides over the Donald Ford Gallery in South Queensferry and has recently published two books with his photographs.

Born: Linlithgow, October 25, 1944.
Signed from: Bo'ness United.
Debut: September 26, 1964, First Division, Hearts 4 Celtic 2.
Appearances: 436. Goals: 188.
International honours: Scotland (3).

DAVE McPHERSON

Dave McPherson may have won most of his medals at Ibrox but there is no doubt that he has had a great influence on the shaping of Hearts during two spells at the club.

His partnership with Craig Levein during the 1987-88 season was the cornerstone on which Hearts built their title challenge and it helped the team finish second to Celtic.

But it was at Rangers that McPherson made his first impact. Signed in 1980 from Gartcosh United, he made his first-team debut in 1982 at the age of 18 and during those early days, his promise was noted, as he was awarded a couple of Scotland Under-21 caps. In September, 1983, he scored four goals in a European Cup-Winners' Cup tie against Valetta in Malta.

Hearts manager, Alex MacDonald, used his own Ibrox connection to prize the defender away from the club and parted with £325,000 in the process.

He scored some great goals that first season but the sweetest must have been at Ibrox that April, when Hearts gained an unlikely 2-1 win. However, the following week, there was a deeply disappointing Scottish Cup semi-final defeat by Celtic, when the team returned to Glasgow and lost two late goals.

The following season, McPherson was one of the leading lights in Hearts' run to the quarter finals of the UEFA Cup and indeed almost scored in the away leg against Bayern Munich.

MacDonald appointed him captain of the team in 1989 and the McPherson-Levein partnership was again prominent as Hearts mounted another serious title challenge but ended up third behind Aberdeen on goal difference.

Under Joe Jordan, McPherson was one of only two ever-presents in the Hearts team that embarked on a memorable 15-match unbeaten run in 1991-92, which had many experts tipping them to finally recapture the league title. Unfortunately, after losing 4-0 at home to Aberdeen in the January, Hearts lost the leadership of the league and never managed to overtake Rangers again.

Jordan was intent on building his own team and money had to be raised. So it was that McPherson went back to Ibrox in June, 1992, for a fee of £1.3 million. During his two spells at Rangers, McPherson won three League Championship medals, one Scottish Cup medal and four League Cup medals.

He returned to Tynecastle in October, 1994, as part of the swap deal that took Alan McLaren to Rangers. His first match was a 2-1 defeat by Hibernian in the Edinburgh derby at Easter Road. Typically, McPherson took some revenge of his own the following January, when he scored in a 2-0 win over Hibs.

McPherson went on to win 27 international caps for Scotland and played in the 1990 World Cup finals in Italy and the 1992 European Championship finals in Sweden.

He left Tynecastle at the end of the 1998-99 season to take up the option of playing in Australia with Carlton.

Born: Paisley, January 28, 1964.
Signed from: Rangers.
Debut: August 8, 1987, Premier Division, Hearts 4 Falkirk 2.
Appearances: 416. Goals: 37.
International honours: Scotland (27).

DAVE MACKAY

I f there was one man who was the driving force behind Hearts' fabulous silver streak in the fifties, it was Dave Mackay. A player who went on to win league and cup medals on both sides of the border and to captain his country, it was evident even from an early age that Mackay had leadership qualities that were second to none.

He won the Scottish Schools' Cup as a 14 year-old with Saughton School in Edinburgh and even in those days showed his competitive instincts. After signing schoolboy forms for Hearts, he was farmed out to Newtongrange Star, where he showed no fear in the tackle against players who had considerably more strength and experience.

His first appearance in a Hearts shirt was in a reserve game at Montrose, which finished 6-6. It was clear that Mackay's career was destined to be something out of the ordinary!

He made his first-team debut just a week before his 19th birthday, at left-half in a 2-1 defeat by Clyde but even if his appearances were limited in that first season, he played a small part in Hearts finishing runners-up in the league to Celtic - their highest placing since 1938.

By the following season, he had all but made the number four shirt his own, as Hearts won their first silverware for almost 50 years - beating Motherwell 4-2 in the League Cup Final in which Mackay gave a typically solid display.

The next season, there was a Scottish Cup triumph to celebrate as Hearts beat Celtic in the final and Mackay was developing into one of the best wing-halves in Scotland. He was stationed in England on national service and travelled up to the final the day before the match. Afterwards, he did not have time to over-indulge in celebrations, as he had to return to his base by the Monday morning.

Dave gave outstanding leadership to the team when he captained Hearts to their first league title of the century in 1957-58 and it even included scoring a rare hat-trick in a 9-1 win over Falkirk halfway through the campaign.

Mackay was disappointed to miss the final five games of the season due to a broken foot and those who knew him, it will come as no surprise to learn that he played a full match against Falkirk, not realising the foot was broken.

Later in his career, Mackay was to suffer two leg breaks in the space of nine months but he fought back to full fitness and surprised doctors with the speed of his courageous return.

When he was at Hearts, Mackay won the first of his 22 international caps - against Spain in 1957 - and he was the essence of 'Braveheart' as he gave his all for his country.

Given how keen a competitor he was, Mackay's most painful international memory was the 9-3 defeat by England at Wembley in 1961. He scored one of Scotland's goals that day but there was not much else worth dwelling upon.

By that stage he had joined Tottenham, after Hearts let him go for £30,000 in 1959 - one of his last acts for Hearts being to lead them to another League Cup in October, 1958.

By Wembley, 1961, he was highly regarded. His pen picture from that England v Scotland game in the match programme read: "The Tottenham powerhouse is the controversial character of the Scottish side. Some want him in - some don't. But the man who went to Tottenham from Hearts can be counted on to play his heart out when he steps into a dark blue shirt. He graduated to the Scottish team through the Under-23 side. He is never slow to come up as a sixth forward and has often grabbed a vital goal. Classed by many as the best wing-half in Britain today."

It would be erroneous to label Mackay as simply a fierce competitor, albeit with a bent for leadership. He was a hugely talented player, who could pass the ball as well as any in the team and who was comfortable on the ball.

Scotland manager, Craig Brown, recently described him as one of the best Scottish players he has seen and similarly, Denis Law once accorded him the accolade of saying: "Mackay made Spurs, just as he made Derby later on in his career." Jimmy Greaves, a former team-mate of Mackay's at Spurs, also remarked that he was the team's best-ever player.

Tottenham were no better than mid-table when Mackay joined them but it was not long before they had won the league and cup double - the first English team to achieve the feat in the 20th century. The team went on to become the first British side to win a European trophy, when they won the European Cup-Winners' Cup in 1963 but Mackay was to miss the final due to a stomach injury.

The player joined Derby in 1968 but could so easily have returned to Hearts had Brian Clough, then manager of the Second Division side, not been so persuasive.

Mackay guided Derby into the First Ddivision and later in his career at the Baseball Ground, was voted joint Player of the Year in England with Manchester City's Tony Book.

During his playing career, Mackay won no fewer than ten winner's medals: one Scottish League, one Scottish Cup, two Scottish League Cup, one English League, three FA Cup, one European Cup-Winners' Cup and one English Second Division.

After his playing days were over, Mackay turned to management and had spells at Swindon, Nottingham Forest and Derby, before leaving for the Middle East, where he had successful stints in Kuwait and Dubai. He currently lives in Nottingham but enjoys the occasional visit to Tynecastle.

Born: Edinburgh, November 14, 1934.
Signed from: Newtongrange Star.
Debut: November 7, 1953, Division One, Hearts 1 Clyde 2
Appearances: 208. Goals: 32.
International honours: Scotland (22).

SANDY CLARK

andy Clark gave Hearts tremendous value for money when he signed from Rangers for just £35,000 back in October, 1984. A forward who was prepared to go in where it hurt, Clark proved the perfect foil for John Robertson when Hearts threatened to get back amongst the silverware in the 1980s.

Born and brought up in Airdrie, he played for his hometown team after leaving school and started as a part-time player. His goals earned him attention from clubs throughout Britain and West Ham persuaded him to join them in 1992 and turn full-time at the age of 25. But he was in London for less than a year before he returned north to sign for Rangers in a £165,000 deal.

Clark was a firm favourite with the Hearts fans from the first day he pulled on a maroon shirt. Standing six-foot tall, he proved a menace for opposing defenders with his aerial ability and Robertson was at his most potent when Clark was there to knock the ball down for him.

On his debut at Cappielow, Clark netted in a 3-2 win (perhaps significantly, Robertson also scored) over Morton and he then scored twice in a 3-2 win at St Mirren three weeks later. It was proving a difficult season for Hearts but Clark had taken over the number nine shirt from Jimmy Bone and by the end of the season, had scored nine times and finished second-top scorer to Robertson.

To further endear him to the Hearts' supporters, Clark had scored a New Year's Day winner over Hibernian and also netted in the April Edinburgh derby, at Tynecastle. If Robertson had a happy knack of scoring on these occasions, then Clark was not far behind. He was to score in two further wins against Hibs the following season and also took this ability to damage Hearts' local rivals into management.

Not only did he guide Hearts to a notable 3-0 win over Hibs at Easter Road in September, 1990, when he was briefly caretaker-manager before Joe Jordan took over but when he was given the reins for real in 1993-94, he ensured Hearts won three and drew two of the five meetings, including a 2-1 Scottish Cup fourth round tie at Easter Road.

The Clark-Robertson partnership was at its most productive in 1985-86, when, with John Colquhoun also scoring valuable goals, Hearts were taken to the brink of the league title.

Hearts made a modest start to the season but by November, when Clark scored twice in a 3-0 win over Rangers at Tynecastle (Robertson nabbed the other goal), their intent was clear.

Rangers were also beaten at Tynecastle the following March - this time 3-1 (Robertson 2, Clark) - and when Hearts won 3-0 at Tannadice against Dundee United in mid-April (Robertson 2, Clark), it looked as if it could be Hearts' year. But the next trip to Tayside three weeks later was to be the end of the title dream, as Hearts lost two goals to Dundee in the final minutes, which cost them the league.

Born: Airdrie, October 28, 1956.
Signed from: Rangers.
Debut: October 20, 1984, Premier League, Morton 2 Hearts 3.
Appearances: 205. Goals: 56.
International honours: 0.

TOMMY JENKINSON

ommy Jenkinson secured his place in Hearts history on April 10, 1886, when he scored Tynecastle's first goal. Hearts had left Old Tynecastle that February and had erected a new grandstand on the current site, at a cost of £200.

To open the new stadium, Hearts invited Bolton Wanderers north and within five minutes of the kick-off, Jenkinson had christened the stadium with its first goal. Hearts went on to win the match 4-1 in front of a crowd of between 5,000-6,000.

Jenkinson, a speedy winger with an eye for goal, also has the distinction of being Hearts' first international player, having been capped by Scotland in 1887 in a match against Ireland at Hampden. Scotland won 4-1 and Jenkinson managed to contribute one of the goals.

Born in April, 1865, he signed for Hearts at the age of 19 in the summer of 1884 and quickly worked his way through the reserves. He received his call-up early, as ten Hearts players had been suspended by the Scottish Football Association for playing professionally. The professional game was frowned upon at the time and 57 Scots had gone south of the border to play for English clubs - ten of them from Tynecastle - and all were banned from playing in Scotland again.

Thus, the young Jenkinson took full advantage and quickly endeared himself to the club's supporters. He played for Hearts in their only excursion into the English FA Cup, when they were beaten 7-1 by Darwen, before the SFA ruled that Scottish clubs could not play in other national associations' competitions.

Jenkinson spent seven years at Tynecastle and scored over 60 goals in his time at the club before he left to join Liverpool. He later emigrated to Australia.

Born: Edinburgh, April, 1865.
Debut: 1884.
Appearances: 100. Goals: 61.
International honours: Scotland (1).

TOM PURDIE

om Purdie was Hearts' first captain and is widely credited with giving the club its name. There are differing versions of how the club was formed in 1874 but it seems certain that it was named after the old jail at the Tolbooth, which was pulled down in 1817. The name of the jail was still fresh at the time due to Sir Walter Scott's novel, 'Heart of Midlothian'.

Purdie, legend has it, gave the name to the new football team that was emerging and he won the captaincy after a one-on-one match with Jake Reid, another prominent player of the time, who lost after putting the ball through his own goal.

Purdie was a towering figure in Hearts' early years and played in defence, at half-back and in attack. The early matches with rivals, Hibernian, proved volatile affairs and Purdie always seemed to be in the thick of things.

Hearts won the Edinburgh Association Cup at Powburn in April, 1878, after four draws between the clubs but after the 3-2 win, Purdie was chased from the pitch to Causewayside by rival fans and it is said that he had to use a cabbie's whip to fend them off.

A year later in the Edinburgh Association Cup, Hearts gained a 1-1 draw in the first match and when Purdie was carried off the field shoulder-high by Hearts supporters, he was stoned and later kicked by Hibs fans and a supporter was arrested by police.

Purdie and Hearts had a great rivalry with Hibs and their captain, Michael Whelahan, who was no less a figure to the new team that had emerged amongst Irish immigrants.

The Hearts captain was a widely respected figure in Edinburgh football circles and although he had finished playing by the time Hearts had won the Scottish Cup for the first time in 1891, he was on Hearts' committee when they next won the trophy, five years later.

"In his day, he was a shining light of Scottish football - as captain for several seasons of the Heart of Midlothian in their famous early days, his name became and is yet, a household word," wrote the 'Edinburgh Athletic Times', after Hearts won the Scottish Cup for a second time in 1896.

"Mr Purdie has followed the club through all its vicissitudes and to him it must have been a special pleasure to think that he was a member of the committee this season, when the team had again won the blue riband of Scottish football.

"Personally, Mr Purdie is a quiet and somewhat reserved gentleman but his judgement is rendered possibly all the sounder because of his discretion."

Born: 1854
Appearances: 50.
International honours: 0.

JIM JEFFERIES

It is likely that Jim Jefferies' contribution to Hearts will be measured more through what he has done as a manager rather than as a player. He was the man who finally brought a major trophy to Tynecastle after a 36-year wait and for that, he is guaranteed Hearts immortality.

Yet, Jefferies has taken many of his strengths as a player into his management career. Known for his inspirational leadership and never-say-die attitude, Jefferies demands the same commitment from his current squad of players.

He replaced Peter Oliver at left-back when he made his debut as a 21 year-old in a 2-2 draw with East Fife at Bayview in March, 1972 and impressed enough to hold his place for the next couple of months.

The following season, he shared the number three shirt with Oliver and the reliable Dave Clunie but he was soon to win a regular place, either at left-back or left-half.

These were barren times for Hearts, although Jefferies played his part in Hearts' marathon Scottish Cup run that year, which ended with a final defeat by Rangers at Hampden.

Jefferies was now an automatic choice and the following season, played in the memorable 5-1 European win over Lokomotiv Leipzig; and if goals were few and far between for the player, there was a rare double in a 2-1 league win over Aberdeen at Tynecastle a few weeks later, in what was Hearts' first league win of that season.

Hearts reached the semi finals of both the League Cup and the Scottish Cup that season but their league form in 1976-77 was poor. At the end of the campaign, they were relegated for the first time in their history.

Jefferies played in all but one of the matches the following season, as Hearts were promoted back to the Premier League behind Morton on goal difference. These were hard times, as Hearts bobbed between the Premier League and the First Division, with captain Jefferies one of the few players to consistently turn in good performances week after week.

There was also the odd goal or two, as Jefferies piled up over 300 appearances for the club. He left the club to join Berwick Rangers - a club he was later to manage - at the age of 32, in 1982.

It was to be almost 13 years before he returned to manage the club he loved but considering he led them to Scottish Cup success less than three years after taking over, the supporters will feel it was worth the wait.

Born: Musselburgh, November 22, 1950.
Signed from: Gorgie Hearts.
Debut: March 4, 1972, First Division, East Fife 2 Hearts 2.
Appearances: 349. Goals: 6.
International honours: 0.

WILLIE WALLACE

herever Willie Wallace played, goals were sure to follow. From his earliest days, when he started out as a teenager at Stenhousemuir, to a rich seam of goals at Tynecastle, Wallace had a happy knack of finding the net. It was a talent that was to win him a European Cup winners' medal as part of the Celtic side that became the first British team to win the trophy in 1967.

In April, 1961, Hearts paid a record fee of £15,000 to bring Wallace to the club from Raith Rovers (where he had moved from Stenhousemuir two years previously). He was to leave just over five years later for £30,000 and within a year had won that European medal as the most expensive member of Jock Stein's 'Lisbon Lions'. He had also won a league medal, Scottish Cup medal and League Cup medal, as Celtic swept the boards.

Wallace provided a healthy scoring return from his 277 games for Hearts, as he notched 158 goals and was top scorer at Tynecastle in every season he was there. Even though he left Hearts in December, 1966, he was still top scorer for the club at the end of that season with nine goals - four of which he scored in a 4-3 League Cup win over Clyde in the August.

He made his debut in April, 1961, in a 2-1 win over Dundee at Tynecastle and, although he never managed to get on the scoresheet, he was on target three days later in a notable 3-1 win at Celtic Park, in what was Hearts' last game of the season.

He was the natural successor to Willie Bauld, who he played with on a handful of occasions in 1961-62 but who was nearing the end of his time at the club.

That season, Wallace managed a dozen goals, to finish ahead of Johnny Hamilton in the scoring stakes by a single goal but his next four seasons - 25, 30, 26, 27 - showed why he was one of the most feared forwards in Scottish football at the time.

Wallace had played in the Hearts sides that lost the League Cup Final to Rangers in 1961, in both the first tie (1-1) and the replay (1-3) but did not manage to find the target.

A year later he eased Hearts into the final again with a hat-trick in a 4-0 semi-final win over St Johnstone at Easter Road. This time, he collected a winners' medal in the narrow 1-0 win over Kilmarnock but it was to be the last medal he won at the club. He was later to win every honour in the domestic game - as well as European success - with Celtic.

His goalscoring exploits won him an international call-up for Scotland in 1965, when he was selected to play against Northern Ireland. He was also chosen to play against England and Holland while still at Tynecastle, in 1966 and went on to bring his cap tally to seven when he moved to Celtic, including playing in the 3-2 win over then world champions, England, at Wembley, in 1967.

Born: Kirkintilloch, 23 June, 1940
Signed from: Raith Rovers.
Debut: April 29, 1960, First Division, Hearts 2 Dundee 1.
Appearances: 277. Goals: 158.
International honours: Scotland (7).

ALEX MASSIE

**A**lex Massie spent just five years at Tynecastle but was a player who commanded respect throughout Europe. Even after he left the club late in 1935 to join Aston Villa, he was known as the 'Ace of Hearts' by followers of the Birmingham club.

Massie, born in Glasgow, played for Partick Thistle, Ayr United and Bury before he had a short time playing in America. It was from Dublin Dolphins that Hearts signed him in 1930 at the age of 24, originally as an inside-forward.

He was later switched to right-half and the emerging Tommy Walker was much influenced by the talents of Massie, who was to earn 11 full international caps for Scotland during his time at Tynecastle, to which seven more were added when he joined Aston Villa.

Massie was a much-respected player for his dribbling skills and also his passing ability and he captained Scotland on several occasions.

He was given a benefit match against Belgrade Sports Club in November, 1935 and before the turn of the year, he had been transferred to Villa for a then substational fee of £6,500.

Massie was to return to Tynecastle at the age of 35 to guest for the team in several wartime matches but by then, his best days were behind him. He eventually took over as manager of Villa in 1945.

Born: Glasgow, 1906.
Signed from: Dublin Dolphins.
Debut: October, 1930.
International honours: Scotland (18).

JOHN ROBERTSON

There has been no greater modern-day goalscorer for Hearts than John Robertson. Having scored goals from his first days in maroon, Robertson set his sights on the league scoring records of the 'Terrible Trio' and, in turn, surpassed Alfie Conn, Willie Bauld and then Jimmy Wardhaugh.

Robertson, who went on to score a league record 214 goals in Hearts' colours, was nabbing goals almost from birth. Even at Parson's Green Primary in Edinburgh, he had built up quite a reputation and by the time he had graduated to Portobello High School, he was attracting attention from major clubs in England and Scotland.

Famously, he could have signed for Hibernian, had the then chairman, Tom Hart, not told him as a teenager that if he did not sign at that moment in his office, he would never play for the club. The young Robertson wanted time to discuss it with his older brother, Chris, then playing for Rangers but when it was denied, he left the contract unsigned and instead, signed for Hearts the next day. Since that day, he punished Hibs more than any other Hearts player - scoring a record 27 goals (26 in the league and one in the Scottish Cup) in Edinburgh derbies.

Capped at schoolboy level for Scotland - he played but did not score in the celebrated 5-4 win over England at Wembley in 1980 - he went on to play 16 times for the full international team. Many experts believe that had he played in an Old Firm shirt, he would have won many more.

Robertson, who curiously never managed a Premier Division hat-trick, though he scored trebles in the First Division and in the cup, was one of the most consistent scorers in the Premier Division and dominated the Hearts scoring charts for long enough.

From 1983-84 to 1996-97, he led the club scoring lists every season bar one - in 1988-89, when he was down at Newcastle for half a season.

In short, Robertson, who stands just 5'6", has a basic instinct for goals. To assess his qualities, there are no better witnesses than those he has played alongside.

Jimmy Bone, who nurtured Robertson through his early years at Hearts, points out: "He has always had a great awareness in the penalty box. His first touch is very good and he was also a very good learner."

Sandy Clark, who Robertson also credits with playing a big part in his development as a striker, adds: "He is a rare breed. The likes of Ally McCoist could score goals all day from 10-12 yards but John can also do it from 20-25 yards. He is also intelligent, reads situations well and has great timing."

Robertson made his debut for Hearts when he came on as a substitute in a match against Queen of the South - by coincidence, the team Bauld made his debut against - and joined his brother Chris. The two played together for the final 17 minutes of the game but it was to be as much as they managed. Chris departed at the end of the season and John did not play another competitive match until the following season.

It was in the summer of 1982 that Robertson notched his first goal for the club, when he scored in a pre-season friendly at Blyth Spartans in front of only 512 spectators.

The goals were to follow by the barrowload over the seasons ahead. Good with both feet, he also scored more than his fair share with his head and when Hearts returned to the Premier Division in 1983, he scored two in a thrilling 3-2 win over Hibs at Tynecastle. He went on to bag 20 goals that season.

His 20 goals in 34 appearances in 1985-86 took Hearts to within touching distance of the league title and there was one memorable strike against Dundee United at Tannadice in the April that was a candidate for 'goal of the season'.

There was another vintage year in 1987-88, when he scored 31 goals and it was little wonder that Newcastle United should lure him south that summer. But Robertson was never really given a chance to show what he could do on Tyneside and he was back at Hearts by December, with the club forking out a record £750,000 for the return of their favourite son. Typically, the first goal at Tynecastle on his return was the winner against Hibs.

The change of managers at Tynecastle in the nineties did not blunt Robertson's sharpness and he had clearly not lost his touch, even after turning 30.

He scored a valuable Scottish Cup semi-final goal in 1996, which helped Hearts into the final for the first time in ten years and the following season, scored against Celtic in extra-time in the League Cup quarter final at Tynecastle. It helped Hearts progress and though there was another final defeat at the hands of Rangers in this competition, Robertson managed to help himself to a goal in the event.

By 1997-98, however, it was clear his days at the top level with Hearts were numbered. Yet, he still managed two more goals against Hibs that season and although he started only ten league matches, he scored half a dozen goals. He was also on the bench in the Scottish Cup Final when he finally secured a winner's medal for his unrivalled service to the club over a period of 16 years. It was part of the plan to bring him on for the final few minutes of the final but with Rangers pressing for an equaliser, Jim Jefferies dared not upset the equilibrium of the team at that stage.

Nonetheless, Robertson, after 720 matches for Hearts, deserved his medal as much as anyone in the team and it was a fitting end to his Tynecastle career. In the close-season, he was to join Livingston as player-coach and he showed at Almondvale that the goals have not dried up.

He scored the winning goal in a shock victory at Aberdeen in the Scottish Cup and added a handful more to help Livingston win promotion to the First Division at the end of the campaign.

Born: Edinburgh, October 2, 1964.
Signed from: Edina Hibs.
Debut: February 17, 1982, Division One, Hearts 4 Queen of the South 1.
Appearances: 720. Goals: 310.
International honours: Scotland (16).

ALFIE CONN

Alfie Conn was the first of the soon-to-be-christened 'Terrible Trio' to sign for Hearts, as a 17 year-old back in 1944, from Inveresk Athletic. He made his debut within four months of signing but it was not until he was joined at the club by Jimmy Wardhaugh and then Willie Bauld that his value to Hearts was appreciated.

An inside-right noted for his strength, pace and thunderous shot, Conn was to make a significant contribution to the 'trio', who scored 952 goals between them in an astonishing period for the club under the management of Davie McLean and then Tommy Walker.

Conn made his debut for Hearts in a 4-0 home win over Dumbarton in October, 1944. In the immediate post-war years, Conn was starting to make a name for himself - he scored in successive wins over Rangers and Aberdeen at the end of the 1946-47 season but it was not until he set foot on the same pitch as Bauld and Wardhaugh - on October 9, 1948, in a 6-1 win over East Fife in the League Cup at Tynecastle, that his career really took off.

He scored twice (Bauld scored a hat-trick and Davie Laing scored the other) and by the end of the season, had finished second-top scorer (behind Bauld, who scored 24) with 17 goals. The goals kept on coming for him and for his two colleagues, although, given the fact he played alongside such prolific scorers, only once did he finish as top scorer - in 1950-51, when he scored 25 goals, two ahead of Bauld and five ahead of Wardhaugh.

Conn was known for his uncanny ability to hang in the air to meet a cross with his head, much in the fashion that Denis Law was noted for some years later. He played in the team that won the League Cup in 1954 by beating Motherwell in the final and in 1956, scored the clinching goal when Hearts won the Scottish Cup by beating Celtic 3-1, to give them the trophy for the first time in 50 years. He was also a member of the team that won the league in 1958, although an ankle injury meant he played in only five matches (though he still scored four goals).

He also had the distinction of scoring Hearts' 100th league goal of the campaign - against Motherwell, at Fir Park, in a 4-0 win. Hearts went on to score 132 goals in the league, in a campaign where the 'Terrible Trio' did not play a single match together, although they did grace the same team in four out of Hearts' six League Cup matches.

Even all these years later, Conn - the last surviving member of the 'Terrible Trio' - does not know the secret of the understanding the threesome had. "I think it was just one of those things that happens in football. We didn't talk about it and in those days, we were all just happy to be in the team and getting a game. We had no idea after that first game against East Fife what we would go on to become together," he recalls.

"I have some great memories of my time at Hearts and we were lucky enough to have a good team. Dave Mackay was also becoming a big influence. He was only a young lad of 16 when I first saw him but he grew up quickly. He was a strong tackler and he could also use strong language if you did something wrong!

"Winning the League Cup was a great feeling, as it was our first trophy for so long and the Scottish Cup was also a tremendous day. I remember coming back to Edinburgh with the trophy and we made a detour via Livingston, as I think the manager, Tommy Walker, wanted to show the cup to his mother. I was from just up the road at Stoneyburn but I don't remember us going past there!"

Conn remembers his initial wage at Tynecastle being just £2 a week but he recollects that there was a bonus of £100 for the Scottish Cup success in 1956.

"That was a lot of money at the time. But I don't think my basic wage went above £16 during my time at Hearts - the game was different from today. Before home games, we would meet for a light meal at Haymarket and then we'd walk to Tynecastle," he continues.

"The main difference between the game now and the game in my day is not just the wages but the speed at which it is played nowadays. But then, the pace of the game in the fifties was a lot faster than it was in the twenties and thirties.

"I don't really go to games these days but then, I never went when I stopped playing. When I was about 25, I was already thinking about what I would do when I gave up the game, as I knew that by the time I was in my early thirties, no-one would want me. Nowadays, I think the top players who are sensible with their money can virtually retire once they finish playing, as the wages are so high."

Conn could not tell you how many appearances or even how many goals he scored for Hearts as, he will explain, he was simply doing his job. But he acknowledges that he was privileged to work with two of the best managers in the game during his time at Hearts.

"For me, Davie McLean was the greatest manager there ever was. Tommy was also a nice man and a good manager but he was quieter. For me, Davie McLean was real class and he knew the game inside-out," he assesses.

Conn confesses that he has never seen Hearts' great modern-day scorer, John Robertson, in the flesh but is an admirer of his achievements. He also took great pride in watching - on television - Hearts' 1998 win in the Scottish Cup ("when you've been a Hearts player, the feeling never leaves you").

Conn's Tynecastle career came to an end in September, 1958, when Raith Rovers paid £2,250 for his services. As he was the first to arrive, he was also the first of the 'trio' to depart - his final game for Hearts coming on April 16, 1958, in a 4-0 win over Aberdeen at Pittodrie, with the league already won.

During his 14 years at the club, Conn scored 221 goals in 408 matches and was capped just once for Scotland - in a 1-1 draw against Austria in 1956. It was an amazing fact that, for all their talents, Conn, Bauld and Wardhaugh could only muster half a dozen caps between them.

"There were a lot of good players around at the time," explained Conn, "Rangers and Celtic also had their share and you could only pick eleven international players. But the teams were selected in Glasgow and I think there was maybe a bit of bias, even if it was unintentional."

Born: Prestonpans, October 2, 1926.
Signed from: Inveresk Athletic.
Debut: October 14, 1944, First Division, Hearts 4 Dumbarton 0.
Appearances: 408. Goals: 221.
International honours: Scotland (1).

JOHN CUMMING

John Cumming can lay claim to more winners' medals in a Hearts shirt than any other player. He played a prominent role as Hearts won seven trophies from 1954-62 under Tommy Walker - a first-team regular during the two Championship-winning seasons of 1958 and 1960 and he also played in the four League Cup-winning teams of the fifties and sixties and in the 1956 Scottish Cup triumph.

This durability came from his high level of physical fitness and it was a surprise to no-one when he went on to become team trainer when his playing days at Tynecastle were over.

He came to Tynecastle as a left-winger but was to make his name as a rugged left-half who was courageous in the tackle and commanding in the air. Cumming would give everything for the cause and that was clearly demonstarted during the 1956 Scottish Cup Final with Celtic, when he suffered a head wound that required four stitches after a clash with Willie Fernie but with no substitutes in those days, elected to play on and help steer Hearts to victory.

"That match was one of the highlights of my time at Hearts. We had a brilliant team in those days and there were 139,339 at Hampden to see the final," he recalls.

"The supporters really had value for money back then. There were a lot of good teams around and the 2-3-5 formation meant that they saw attacking football week-in, week-out.

"We had crowds of 30,000-40,000 at Tynecastle for big matches and we had good players in every position. The competition for places was so great that, even if you had a slight injury, you did not want to let it be known, as you knew someone could come in and take your place and you might not get it back.

"Even someone like Willie Bauld struggled to get his game at one point and we had players like Alex Young, who could play different positions in the forward-line and could fill in for anyone."

Cumming, brought up in Carluke, spent so much time playing the game that he did not actually see a professional match until he was 19. It was shortly after that that he joined Hearts and he made his debut in December, 1950, in a 2-2 draw with Celtic at Parkhead, when Jimmy Wardhaugh scored twice.

He kept his place for the rest of that season on the left wing, with Davie Laing occupying the left-half berth. He even managed four goals in that first season, his first coming in a league game against Third Lanark in February, 1951, which Hearts won 4-0.

Cumming played in a fertile forward-line, which was made up by Tommy Sloan, Alfie Conn, Willie Bauld, Jimmy Wardhaugh and himself and while he also played at inside-left in those early days, it was when he dropped back deeper that Hearts went on to enjoy the best years in their history.

"It was a great team to play in. When we won the league in 1958, we scored 132 goals and only lost 29. We only lost one match and that was to Clyde and we drew four," Cumming goes on.

"While it was true that we had some tremendous players, I think one of the secrets of our success at the time was that we were very fit. The credit for that must go to our trainer, John Harvey. I call him 'Mr Hearts' as he gave so much to the club and he looked after the team, whereas Tommy Walker was more the secretary-manager and we didn't see a lot of him during the week.

"Mr Harvey took us for three weeks for stamina training at Gullane before the season and that gave us a great fitness base. After that, the rest was just sharpening up and although players today have to be very fit, that Hearts team would have matched up well."

Cumming was appointed captain and Hearts went on to more glory, winning the league again in 1960, by just four points from Kilmarnock, with the wing-half playing in all but two of the league fixtures and contributing a valuable five goals.

By that stage, the 'Terrible Trio' had split up, with Conn and Wardhaugh having departed but Bauld was still scoring regularly for the club. Like many, Cumming - who went on to win nine international caps for Scotland after making his debut against Hungary - believes that the 'trio' should have been given more opportunities to play for their country.

"Willie Bauld was a very shy person. I used to pick him up every day to go to training when I drove from Carluke and he did not come across as the most confident. But that changed the moment he stepped onto a football pitch and he expressed himself better when he played," he points out.

Cumming's last medal at Hearts came in the 1962 League Cup, when he was the most experienced member of the team that beat Kilmarnock 1-0 thanks to a Norrie Davidson goal but by then, he was also combining playing with coaching.

However, he was still registered as a player and Hearts recalled him for two unexpected games midway through the 1966-67 season at the age of 36, when he played against Aberdeen and Dunfermline but he had no desire to go on any longer. During his remarkable career, in which he was known as hard but fair, he was never once booked.

Coaching was proving the priority and he also worked with the Scotland international squad under Bobby Brown but he later gave that up to devote his full attention to Hearts. He worked under John Harvey, Bobby Seith and John Hagart and as player and coach, he spent almost 27 years at Tynecastle.

He left the club in 1976 and understandably, still maintains a keen interest in their fortunes. "I was at Celtic Park in 1998 when they won the Scottish Cup and that was a special day. I was offered the chance to travel back to Edinburgh on the team bus but unfortunately, I had other commitments, but I enjoyed the occasion," he reveals.

"I still regularly go to games and there are still good players around. The key to it is to work hard and believe in yourself, without being big-headed. I would like to see more young Scottish players getting the chance now.

"I think clubs nowadays tend to throw them in for two or three matches without giving them the chance to develop. In my day, players were given the opportunities but now it seems as if foreign players are preferred to the home-grown ones, which is a shame."

Born: Carluke, March 17, 1930.
Signed from: Carluke Rovers.
Debut: December 30, 1950, First Division, Celtic 2 Hearts 2.
Appearances: 612. Goals: 58.
International honours: Scotland (9).

JOHN CUMMING WITH CUP

BOB MERCER

It has been reported that Bob Mercer was the finest centre-half in Scotland before the First World War and the sturdy, 6'1" defender was renowned for his ability in the air and thoughtful distribution.

Mercer began his football career in the Borders and signed with Selkirk before joining Leith Athletic as a teenager. His potential was quickly spotted and Hearts paid Leith a fee of £100 for his services in the summer of 1909.

He soon became a regular in the Hearts team and impressed with his whole hearted approach to the game and commitment to the cause.

Mercer went on to play over 300 matches for the club and scored 37 goals but his contribution would have been much greater but for the advent of war.

He also played at wing-half for the team and went on to win his first international honour when he was selected to play for the Scottish League against the Football League at the age of 22. Mercer was to go on and win two full international caps - against Wales in 1912 and Ireland in 1913 - but he would surely have gone on to win many more international honours had it not been for the First World War.

It was widely acknowledged that Hearts had one of the best teams in Scotland at the time but the war robbed them of the league title in season 1914-15. Hearts led the league but when the entire squad volunteered to serve their country in November, 1914, the way was left clear for Celtic to go on and snatch the League Championship.

Mercer saw active service in Flanders but suffered gas poisoning at the River Somme in 1918. He looked to have made a full recovery when he led Hearts to the Victory Cup Final in 1919 but it soon became obvious his health was deteriorating as a result of his wartime experiences.

A benefit game was arranged in August, 1919, against a Glasgow Select, which attracted a crowd of around 13,000. Mercer then contracted pneumonia and was seriously ill for a few months.

Hearts retired the popular player in 1921 but he was determined to play on and played for a couple of seasons with Dunfermline before returning to Tynecastle to take on a scouting and coaching role.

It was on April 23, 1926, when he took a Hearts team to play Selkirk at Ettrick Park that he decided to make a guest appearance against the team he started out with. However, during the match, he collapsed and died as a result of heart failure at the age of just 37.

Born: Avonbridge, 1889.
Signed from: Leith Athletic.
Debut: 1909.
Appearances: 317. Goals: 37.
International honours: Scotland (2).

ALEX YOUNG

When Hearts won the league title twice in three years - in 1958 and 1960 - it was Alex Young who supplied more goals than any other player in maroon. Young, born in Loanhead and signed for Hearts from junior club, Newtongrange Star, scored 24 league goals in 1957-58 and 23 in 1959-60.

He was capped half a dozen times at Under-23 level and went on to win eight full caps - six of which were during his days at Hearts. He made his debut in a League Cup win over Partick Thistle in August, 1955, as a replacement for Willie Bauld and scored the winning goal. The 18 year-old had quite an impact as Hearts won their League Cup section - he scored a hat-trick in a 4-0 win over East Fife and was also on the scoresheet against Raith Rovers.

Young went on to score 23 goals in that first season and was part of the team that won the Scottish Cup with a 3-1 win over Celtic at Hampden in the April - the first time the trophy had been brought back to Tynecastle for 50 years.

By then, he had established himself as an important member of the forward line with his dazzling skills and he was a firm favourite with the Tynecastle fans. He was to be prominent in the title success of 1958 with 24 league goals in 34 appearances and he scored the goal that clinched the league at St Mirren. He missed the League Cup win over Partick Thistle in 1958 but scored the winning goal in the 2-1 win over Third Lanark in the final the following year, in a season when Hearts went on to win the league again.

He netted many crucial goals in that campaign - none more so than the second in a 2-0 win over title-chasing Rangers in early March, when he took a pass from Johnny Hamilton to calmy find the net. As in 1958, the title was secured at St Mirren - this time in a thrilling 4-4 draw, when Bauld scored the final goal that was enough to give Hearts the solitary point they needed. As in 1958, Young also found the net that day, when he scored twice, although his first was initially credited to Jim McFadzean.

Young's move to Everton along with George Thomson - for £42,000 - provoked a storm of protest from Hearts' supporters, who made their feelings known during the match against Raith Rovers at Tynecastle a few days later. Young had gone to Merseyside with a knee injury and did not play for three months. When he made his debut, it was ironically against Dave Mackay's Tottenham Hotspur - Mackay having left Tynecastle some 15 months before Young. But Young was to go on to become a firm favourite with the Everton fans and played in the team that won the FA Cup with a 3-2 win over Sheffield Wednesday in 1966, having also won a League Championship medal with the Merseyside club three years earlier.

His international career had also blossomed. He had a quiet game on his debut against England in 1960 but played in five more matches that year and scored in the games against Hungary, Turkey and Northern Ireland. His final two caps - against the Republic of Ireland in 1961 and Portugal in 1966 - came when he was an Everton player.

He left Everton in 1968 to join Glentoran in Northern Ireland and also had a stop at Stockport in the English Third Division before a knee injury hastened his retirement.

His son, Jason, followed him into the professional game and was to sign for Hearts in 1988. Young junior also played with Livingston before signing for Stranraer.

Born: Loanhead, February 3, 1937.
Signed from: Newtongrange Star.
Debut: August 27, 1955, League Cup, Hearts 2 Partick Thistle 1.
Appearances: 249. Goals: 150.
International honours: Scotland (8).

GARY LOCKE

Some would have you believe that Gary Locke is one of the unluckiest players to have played for Hearts in recent times. Elevated to the position of club captain before his 21st birthday under Jim Jefferies, he has been around when Hearts have played in three cup finals. Yet, except for seven minutes, he has been a spectator at all three.

Locke, himself, does not see it that way. He has experienced more than his share of injuries but it is still early in his career and given that he has played more than 180 matches for Hearts so far and is one of the longest-serving players at the club, it is easy to assume that he is older than he is.

Given his chance as a 17 year-old by then manager, Sandy Clark, Locke made his debut when he came on as a substitute in an end-of-season game against St Johnstone at McDiarmid Park.

By the start of the following season, the remarkable maturity he showed for his years persuaded Clark that he should be given the right-back slot from the day the campaign opened at Ibrox.

Locke never let his manager down and went on to play 39 matches for the club that season. If the departure of Clark meant that Locke had to bide his time in the reserve team the following season when Tommy McLean was in charge, then there was no doubt that he would get another opportunity.

With Jefferies content to give the young players at Tynecastle a chance, Locke was back in favour in 1995-96. A player of boundless energy who always gives a hundred per cent, he has proved a natural leader at Hearts.

Deployed at right-back or in midfield, his ability to cover every inch of turf has been a hallmark of his game. If it is his energetic style and tough tackling that have earned him respect throughout the Premier League, his ability to make precise passes behind defences is a part of his game that is often overlooked.

There was never any doubt that Locke would end up at Tynecastle from an early age, as he used to stand on the terraces as a youth and even when he had lengthy spells out of the team through injury, he could be found in the stands back amongst the supporters.

Yet it is a little-known fact that Locke, like John Robertson, trained with Hibernian as a youngster and could have ended up playing at Easter Road had things worked out differently for him.

"All of my family were Hearts daft and my dad was a season-ticket holder. I first went along with him to watch matches when there were players like Frank Liddell and Willie Pettigrew playing," he explains.

"Hearts were in the First Division at the time and we went to places like Queen of the South or Montrose. Then, John Robertson and Gary Mackay broke into the team and they were my heroes.

"I was first spotted by Hearts when I was playing with Hutchison Vale. We were playing in a tournament at Grangemouth and Ian Grassick, the Hearts scout at the time, watched me.

"I had been training with a number of clubs, including Hibs and I kept waiting for Hearts to contact me to tell me to come and train with them; but it looked as if it was never going to happen.

"I was getting a lot of stick from my dad, as I was training at Hibs every Tuesday night. I was asked to go and train with Rangers and Celtic but once Hearts came in, there was no other option for me.

"I trained there from Under-10 level until I was 16 and then I was taken onto the ground staff. It was Alex MacDonald who first signed me but just when I started, Joe Jordan took over and so there was some uncertainty about my future.

"Sandy Clark then gave me my big break when he took over as manager. I have nothing but the utmost respect for him and he has helped make me the player I am today.

"It was a great family occasion when I played my first match for the club. It was against St Johnstone at McDiarmid Park on the last day of the season in 1992-93.

"I was substitute the previous week against Airdrie and getting on against St Johnstone was a big moment for me and the rest of my family. We lost 3-1 but I can hardly remember anything about the game as it went so quickly."

Locke admits that his Scottish Cup Final experience in 1996 is the lowest point of his career so far. "There was a big build-up to the final and to be captain that day was a great thrill for me. All my family and friends were there and then, seven minutes into the game, I go down with a serious knee injury," he explains.

"It took me a long time to get over that but I'm back now and it was a great day when we went on to win the cup in 1998. I was frustrated not to play that day but to watch Hearts for so long without them winning anything meant it was still a special day to watch them finally do it."

Locke was still out because of injury in November 1996 when Hearts lost in the League Cup Final to Rangers, this time by the tighter margin of 4-3 and there were signs that Hearts' day in the sun would not be delayed for too much longer.

Gary made his comeback in January 1997, ironically in the first match in Hearts' next Scottish Cup campaign. Fortunately, he came through the 5-0 third round win over Cowdenbeath with no adverse reaction and he kept his place, although the cup run ended this time in the next round after a replay with Dundee United.

He played only 21 league matches the following year but, having missed the dramatic cup semi-final win over Falkirk at Ibrox, there was fresh hope he could make the final when he started a game against Rangers at the end of that month. But in the build-up to the cup final, it became obvious that he would be sidelined again.

Nevertheless, he was able to share in the triumph as Steve Fulton, who assumed the captain's mantle on the day, did not hoist the Scottish Cup until Locke had made his way from the stand to the pitch to share the moment with him.

Locke has been capped at Under-21 level for Scotland and a full international honour will surely follow if he can continue to display the maturity he has shown at club level.

Born: Edinburgh, June 16, 1975.
Signed from: Whitehill Welfare.
Debut: May 15, 1993, Premier Division, St Johnstone 3 Hearts 1.
Appearances: 180. Goals: 11.
International honours: 0.

ALEX MacDONALD

lex MacDonald's influence on Hearts, as a player and as a manager, was considerable. He arrived at the club as a player in August 1980 for a £30,000 fee from Rangers, where he had been widely respected. A member of the Rangers team that won the European Cup-Winners' Cup in 1972, MacDonald had also been capped once for Scotland in a 1976 international against Switzerland at Hampden Park, when Willie Pettigrew, later to play at Tynecastle, scored the only goal.

MacDonald, who had played with St Johnstone before joining Rangers, arrived at Tynecastle when the club was in some turmoil but when he left, ten years later, Hearts were in a much healthier state.

On and off the field of play, the one thing guaranteed from MacDonald was total commitment. As a player in midfield, he was tigerish in the tackle but could also pass the ball with precision and the fact he could chip in with the odd goal or two, made the £30,000 then manager, Bobby Moncur, paid for him, one of his shrewdest investments.

It was not the best of times when MacDonald arrived. He made his debut in a 3-2 defeat by Partick Thistle at Firhill in front of a crowd of only 4,000 on Hearts' return to the Premier Division after a one-year absence. He took over the captaincy from Jim Jefferies but even his leadership could not turn the tide.

By the end of the season, little had improved and Hearts finished bottom of the heap and were relegated again. At least the season highlighted just how much work had to be done to turn it around at Tynecastle and Wallace Mercer won the power struggle for control of the club. Tony Ford, who had succeeded Moncur as manager, lasted only five months and in January, 1982, MacDonald was given the role of player-manager. Hearts missed out on promotion by just one point but the new manager was proving himself astute in the transfer market and he was soon to turn it around.

Hearts secured promotion the following season as runners-up to St Johnstone and MacDonald's blend of youth and experience took the Premier Division by storm. His team won their first five league matches - including notable victories over Hibs and Rangers. MacDonald went on to play 180 games for the club and scored 20 goals but he soon decided to hang up his boots and concentrate on making his mark as a manager.

He took Hearts back into Europe in 1984 (the first time since 1976) and of course, to the verge of the Premier Division title in 1986. His investment in the transfer market was limited, yet he managed to get the best out of his players and fostered a camaraderie in his squad that was to serve Hearts well.

He guided Hearts to second in the league again in 1988 and to third (behind Aberdeen on goal difference) in 1990 but he was sacked in September, 1990 after the 3-1 home defeat by Rangers, to be succeeded by Joe Jordan.

MacDonald went on to success as manager of Airdrie - taking them to two Scottish Cup Finals - and many of the players who found themselves working under MacDonald were those who had played under him at Hearts.

Born: Glasgow, March 17, 1948.
Signed from: Rangers.
Debut: August 9, 1980, Premier Division, Partick Thistle 3 Hearts 2.
Appearances: 181. Goals: 21.
International honours: Scotland (1).

GARY MACKAY

If the name 'Walker' has played an important part in the growth of Hearts, then in more recent times the name 'Mackay' has loomed large. Dave Mackay, of course, was the driving force behind the team that enjoyed such supremacy in the fifties and if Gary Mackay did not have a winners' medal to show for his 17 years at the club, his mark was just as indelible.

The midfield player, who made his debut as a 16 year-old in a League Cup tie at Somerset Park, went on to play a club record 515 league games - a total that will surely never be surpassed, given the way the game has gone under Bosman - and reach a staggering 737 games for Hearts in all competitions - also a club record.

Having warmed the bench on three or four occasions, Mackay had his first start for the club he had supported as a schoolboy during a Scottish Cup match at Morton, where Hearts secured a creditable 0-0 draw. Unfortunately for Hearts and Mackay, the replay was lost 3-1 at Tynecastle and it was to sum up a miserable season, as Hearts finished bottom of the Premier League and were relegated for the third time in five seasons.

"John Robertson, Ian Westwater, Dave Bowman and myself all signed at around the same time. Hearts did not have a great youth set-up at the time and the first time I walked through the doors at Tynecastle was when I signed for Bobby Moncur," recalls Mackay.

"At school, I had been training with Manchester United, Celtic and like John Robertson, Hibs. Hibs had a big youth set-up and many of the best young players trained with them.

"It pleased my dad, Peter, as he was a Hibs fan but I had always wanted to play for Hearts, as I'd supported them from the terracing. But they were hard times for the club initially, although it gave me a good grounding in the game.

"Alex MacDonald and Sandy Jardine introduced a new professionalism when they joined and they proved to be a big influence on my career. Jimmy Bone and Sandy Clark also helped me immensely, as did Willie Johnston. Many people misjudged Willie because of his disciplinary record but he was a magnificent professional and I still keep in touch with him to this day.

"George McNeill and Bert Logan, the fitness coaches at Tynecastle, also had a big influence on me, as they gave me a good level of fitness from an early age and that stood me in good stead for the rest of my career and allowed me to play for as long as I did."

Mackay was soon a fixture in the Hearts team and was guided through his early days by the wily MacDonald, before the former Rangers midfield player retired to the manager's office at Tynecastle.

He quickly built up an almost telepathic understanding with Robertson and his ability to break from midfield, run at defenders and play accurate passes at pace was a feature of the Mackay game. He also had an eye for a goalscoring opportunity, himself and had the knack of scoring spectacular goals.

When Hearts won promotion to the Premier Division in 1983, they won their first five league games and went on to clinch a place in the following season's UEFA Cup with a mixture of veterans and youngsters.

In 1986, Mackay's incisive and perceptive play helped Hearts to the brink of the League Championship and a spectacular goal which settled victory against Clydebank at Tynecastle in late April brought the title within grasp. But it was to be the last goal Hearts scored that season - a 2-0 defeat at Dens Park cost them the league and the following Saturday, a 3-0 loss to Aberdeen in the Scottish Cup Final closed off the other avenue for silverware.

"I was devastated by the events of that week," Mackay confesses. "To lose two matches of such importance within a week was hard to take. Because I was still relatively young, I thought that more chances would come along before too long but then we went through a spell where we lost quite a few semi finals. It taught me that you have to take these chances when they come as you may never get them again in your career."

But Mackay's consistent play won him international recognition with then-manager, Andy Roxburgh, who had been in charge of the Scotland youth team when Mackay was a member, giving him his first cap in a European Championship qualifier against Bulgaria in Sofia in 1987. Scotland were already out of contention but Mackay came on as a substitute and scored the only goal of the game in the closing moments - a wonderfully-executed goal, which had an echo of Kenny Dalglish and which denied Bulgaria a place in the 1988 European finals.

Mackay's goal gave the Irish a place and it proved the renaissance of Irish football under Jack Charlton. Mackay received a crate of Irish whiskey for his effort and the Scottish Football Association were sent a crate of champagne by their Irish counterparts but Mackay notes, no bottle arrived for him from Park Gardens.

"It was a great moment for me. I can't remember much about the goal but it was an honour for me to get my first cap as I was the first Hearts player to be selected for Scotland since Donald Ford in 1974 and I was the first to score since Alex Young 27 years earlier," he remembers. Mackay - who beat John Robertson to a cap - went on to play four times for his country (also against Luxembourg, Saudi Arabia and Malta) but there were no more international goals.

At club level, honours were to elude Mackay but he scored many valuable goals through the years and gave oustanding service to the club. Even as his playing days at Tynecastle were coming to a close, there were two more cup final appearances for him.

He was to play in every round, including the final, as Hearts reached Hampden again for the 1996 Scottish Cup Final under Jim Jefferies, ten years after the huge anti-climax of 1986. There was to be no happy ending this time, either as Hearts lost 5-1 to Rangers and Mackay was to be further disappointed the following season, as Rangers again beat Hearts, this time in the final of the League Cup but only after a terrific battle, which ended 4-3 in the Ibrox side's favour.

Mackay, who had also helped out in the commercial department during his latter days at Tynecastle, finally severed his link with Hearts in March, 1997, when he joined Alex MacDonald at Airdrie, where he was to go on to be assistant manager and then, after MacDonald's departure, manager.

However, there is still a strong bond with Tynecastle. He attended the 1998 Scottish Cup Final, when Hearts finally ended 36 years without a trophy. "It was a tremendous day, as I knew what the Hearts players and supporters were feeling. But I have to admit to feeling slightly jealous that I had not been part of it when Hearts finally won something," Mackay admits.

"It was not resentment or anything like that—just a slight jealousy, as it would just have been something to have still been at Hearts when they did it. I knew what it meant to everyone connected with the club and it was a great day for the club."

Born: Edinburgh, January 23, 1964.
Signed from: Salvesen BC.
Debut: September 24, 1980, League Cup, Ayr United 4 Hearts 0.
Appearances: 737. Goals: 88.
International honours: Scotland (4).

DREW BUSBY

Drew Busby is remembered with affection by Hearts supporters. This bustling forward was one of the most popular Hearts players of the seventies, if his direct approach and scoring power hardly endeared him to opposing defenders.

Brought up in Dunbartonshire, he started his senior career with Coventry City but things did not work out and he soon returned to Scotland to play for Third Lanark. He also had a spell playing junior football before Airdrie signed him and he made a name for himself after striking up a successful scoring partnership with Drew Jarvie.

Hearts paid £35,000 for his services in the summer of 1973 and almost immediately, Busby struck up a rapport with Donald Ford up front. The two scored 45 goals between them in that first season, as Hearts finished sixth in the old First Division. He also scored the only goal of a game at Goodison Park, when Hearts defeated Everton in the first round of the Texaco Cup. Hearts also reached the semi finals of the Scottish Cup that season before losing to Dundee United after a replay.

Busby was good in the air, had a ferocious shot and linked well with his team-mates. He could also play in midfield but it was in attack that he was at his best. He scored 15 goals and again finished second-top scorer behind Donald Ford in the last year of the old first division as Hearts confirmed their place in the new Premier Division with an eighth-place finish.

In 1975-76, he finished joint-top scorer with Willie Gibson - both players managing 15 goals - and he played his part in helping Hearts reach the Scottish Cup Final that year, when he scored in the 3-0 semi-final replay win over Dumbarton. He played in the final against Rangers but it was an unhappy afternoon for Hearts, as they never recovered after conceding an early goal and ended up losing 3-1.

Busby continued to score goals and notched one in the famous 5-1 European Cup-Winners' Cup victory over Lokomotiv Leipzig at Tynecastle in September, 1976 and also scored one of Hearts' goals in the 4-2 defeat by Hamburg in Germany in the following round.

Along with Willie Gibson, on Christmas Eve, 1977, he scored a hat-trick in a 7-0 win over Arbroath and as part of a sponsor's prize, earned a crate of whisky. Hearts regained their top-flight place at the end of the season, as they finished second to Morton on goal difference, with Busby scoring 19 goals in the course of the campaign.

When the club was relegated again at the end of the 1978-79 season, Busby was allowed to leave at the age of 31, after six years at the club and some 84 competitive goals.

After leaving Hearts, he had a time in Canada with Toronto Blizzards and when he returned, also played for Morton and Queen of the South.

Born: Glasgow, December 8, 1947.
Signed from: Airdrie.
Debut: August 11, 1973, League Cup, Hearts 2 Partick Thistle 0.
Appearances: 277. Goals: 90.
International honours: 0.

WILLIE BAULD

o player in the long history of Heart of Midlothian Football Club has been feted more than Willie Bauld. Ask any Hearts supporter, even of the modern generation, who was the 'King of Hearts' and they will give Bauld's name without hestitation.

If what archive film remains of the great goalscorer's talents fails to capture Bauld's achievements, word of mouth from grandfathers has ensured that his name is still held in the highest of esteem today.

Three Scotland international caps do not do justice to his career but then injuries were to hit him hard and he was also unfortunate to be competing for an international place with Lawrie Reilly, the great Hibernian forward who went on to win 38 caps.

At the height of what was dubbed 'the chocolate box controversy' - which centre to choose - Bauld stated: "I can't help admiring Lawrie Reilly. True, he has been chosen at times for Scotland when I thought I might have made the grade but his tremendous dash and energy in front of goal, his tenacity and will to fight for apparent lost causes have impressed me as much as any other follower of the game."

Bauld - and his co-conspirators in the Hearts forward line, Alfie Conn and Jimmy Wardhaugh - only managed half a dozen caps between them, with Conn capped just once and Wardhaugh twice. Considering they shared 950 goals for Hearts, it appears scant recognition.

The late Jock Stein, then manager of Dunfermline and later manager of Scotland, was as astute an observer as any in the Scottish game and he believed Bauld should have been given more opportunities at international level. "Willie never had sufficient full international chances to prove his worth," Stein wrote in 1962 in a booklet to celebrate Bauld's 16 years at Tynecastle. "Of all the centre-forwards since the war, he was the most natural for his position. "His head-work was immaculate. Bauld was as dangerous off the ball as he was on it. His positional sense and anticipation were uncanny. He played it hard, accepted it hard and kept opposing defences busy. It is unlikely his feats and brilliance will ever be forgotten."

Born in the mining village of Newcraighall on the outskirts of Edinburgh, Bauld played for his school team and his Boys' Brigade side before being recruited by Edinburgh Waverley and then Musselburgh Union. He also signed for Musselburgh Athletic, although he never played a game for them.

The young Bauld had many admirers from both north and south of the border and had fate not intervened, he could have made his name at Sunderland and not at Tynecastle. Bauld admitted he was signing more forms than he cared to remember when he was a teenager and - in 1946 - he put pen to paper on a provisional deal with Sunderland that promised him a wage of £5 a week. Fortunately for Hearts, the deal could never be formalised and it was the quick-thinking of the then secretary at Tynecastle, Jimmy Kean, that managed to steer Bauld to the club he had always supported.

The manager at the time was Dave McLean, who famously recruited all three of the 'Terrible Trio' - Conn, Wardhaugh and Bauld - for a total outlay of just £200 and he could hardly have envisaged what his new recruits would go on to achieve. But, regardless of reputations, players had to earn their place in the first-team at Hearts and even Bauld had to serve a two-and-a-half year apprenticeship. He was farmed out to Newtongrange Star and Edinburgh City before he made his first-team debut for Hearts, just three months short of his 21st birthday. He later admitted that, while he was depressed at the thought of being sent to lesser clubs, it was to be a great learning process which was to serve him well in future years. When the day arrived when he could finally pull that maroon shirt over his head, it was obvious he had been straining at the leash. He could hardly have marked his arrival in more dramatic style - scoring a hat-trick in both of his first two matches for the club!

The debut came on October 9, 1948, at Tynecastle, where Bauld, Conn and Wardhaugh played together for the first time against East Fife in the League Cup. Within 14 minutes, Bauld had opened his account and the hat-trick was completed in the second-half with further goals in the 64th and 74th minutes. Conn also scored two that day in a 6-1 win. Queen of the South were next to suffer, as Bauld fired in another hat-trick the following week at Tynecastle in a 4-0 win.

Word was spreading fast that Hearts had found a triumvirate in attack that could end their long, barren spell without a trophy. Bauld finished the season as top scorer with 24 goals, Conn scored 16 and Wardhaugh 14. Between them, the three contributed more than half of Hearts' total for the season.

It was in 1950 that Bauld won his three international caps for Scotland - against England, Switzerland and Portugal - and if there were no more to follow in the years ahead, at least Bauld could content himself with a rush of silver at club level.

Under manager, Tommy Walker, Hearts were to win seven trophies in nine years after 48 years without silverware. Hearts beat Motherwell 4-2 in the final at Hampden to win the League Cup in 1954 and end the famine. Bauld, who had scored nine goals to help Hearts into the final, blasted Motherwell away with a glorious hat-trick. He scored twice within the first 15 minutes and completed the treble with Hearts' fourth goal two minutes from the end.

The welcome Hearts received when returning to Edinburgh with the cup was tumultuous and Bauld was the centre of attraction. The Scottish Cup was the next trophy in Hearts' sights, having not won the competition since 1906.

The greatest prize of all - the League Championship - was won in 1958, with Hearts losing only once and scoring a record 132 goals in 34 matches. Remarkably, Bauld was to score only five of those, as he made just nine appearances in Hearts' first title win for 61 years. When Hearts regained the title two years later, he played in only half of the 34 games but he managed ten goals.

Bauld had been accused of being laid-back in his approach to the game but his contemporaries always argued that his work-rate was first-class. It was just that he had the ability to drift through games and seize the moment when it came. Off the field, he was quiet-living and modest.

"In my career, I've been called a lone wolf because I've never been an enthusiast for social occasions," he explained at the time. "The truth is that I find great relaxation and comfort by my own fireside. As a learner at the game, football was not a much discussed subject at our house. Now, after marriage, the position is unchanged. I think it is good to forget the job once in a while."

In his 16 years at Tynecastle between 1948-62, Bauld scored 355 goals in 510 appearances, 183 of which came in just 292 league games. His last goal came in a 2-1 win over Third Lanark in February, 1962. He was honoured with a testimonial game against Sheffield United that drew a crowd of 15,000 in November, 1962.

But it was an occasion tinged with some bitterness as, when Bauld received his cheque, the price of the match ball and other expenses were deducted. It was to be 12 years before the player returned to Tynecastle.

Sadly, Bauld died prematurely in 1977, only months before Wardhaugh, when he collapsed after attending a supporters' function. The news stunned Edinburgh but 'the King's' achievements will live forever.

Born: Newcraighall, January 24, 1928.
Signed from: Musselburgh Union.
Debut: October 9, 1948, League Cup, Hearts 6 East Fife 1.
Appearances: 510. Goals: 355.
International honours: Scotland (3).

GORDON MARSHALL

ordon Marshall was to gather a considerable medal haul during his time at Tynecastle as he went on to play in two League Championship-winning teams and also three League Cup-winning sides.

If goalkeeper, Wilson Brown, thought he would have no competition for the goalkeeper's jersey when Willie Duff went south for National Service in the 1950s, he was much mistaken. Even at the age of 17, it was clear Marshall had ability and it was at that tender age that he was blooded in the first-team by Tommy Walker.

He made his debut in a 3-2 win over Kilmarnock and kept his place for another handful of matches before Brown took over again. But there was no keeping the youngster out and he went on to play eleven games that season in a campaign that saw Hearts finish just two points behind champions, Rangers.

The following season, Marshall was to play a much more prominent role as Hearts secured the title with 13 points to spare over second-placed Rangers. Much has been written about the goalscoring of this title-winning team - an astonishing 132 in 34 league matches - but it has also to be remembered that only 29 goals were conceded in what was by far the best defensive record in the First Division.

Marshall played in 31 of the 34 league games and kept 13 clean sheets, including a spell where he had four successive shut-outs and only lost three goals in nine matches.

The goalkeeper played in Hearts' first-ever European tie - a 5-1 defeat by Standard Liege in Belgium in the European Cup in September, 1958 - and the following month, added another medal to his growing collection, as Hearts beat Partick Thistle 5-1 at Hampden in the League Cup Final.

Marshall played in all but one of Hearts' 46 games in 1959-60, when again the League Cup was won - this time with a 2-1 win over Third Lanark - and the team regained the league title, this time with four points to spare over Kilmarnock.

Marshall won another medal - and kept a clean sheet - in the 1962 final against Kilmarnock, which Hearts won through a goal from Norrie Davidson. Yet the victory was laced with some controversy, as Kilmarnock felt they had scored a legitimate equalising goal through Frank Beattie, when Marshall was beaten in the final minute. But referee Tom Wharton disallowed the goal.

It was to be Marshall's last season at Hearts and remarkably, the last trophy the club was to win for 36 years. The goalkeeper had spent seven profitable years at Tynecastle but with Cruickshank proving more than able when given his chance, Hearts felt they could accept an offer of £18,000 for their number one. The goalkeeper had played 338 matches for the club and recorded a respectable 84 shut-outs.

Marshall was later to play for Hibernian and Celtic before retiring from the game. His sons, Gordon and Scott, have both made a mark in the professional game, the former as a goalkeeper who has gone on to play for Scotland and the latter as a central defender.

Born: Farnham, July 2, 1939.
Signed from: Dalkeith Thistle.
Debut: November 17, 1956, First Division, Hearts 3 Kilmarnock 2.
Appearances: 338.
International honours: 0.

HENRY SMITH

Tony Ford was not manager of Hearts for long but one of his legacies was Henry Smith. Brought to the club for an outlay of just £2,000 to Leeds United, he was to prove the goalkeeper the club had sought since the departure of Jim Cruickshank four years earlier.

Smith, born in Lanarkshire but brought up in Yorkshire, had worked as a miner before being taken on by Leeds, where he kept some impressive company, as he was at the club at the same time as David Harvey, David Stewart, David Seaman and John Lukic. It was little wonder he could not force his way into the first team.

If few had heard of Smith when he arrived at Tynecastle, he was to make a considerable mark, as he spent 15 years at the club and set a new club shut-out record in the league with 171 clean sheets and went on to play for Scotland on three occasions.

Smith started with a clean sheet - a 1-0 win at Airdrie in the League Cup in August, 1981 - and he followed up with another shut-out when Hearts beat Aberdeen by an identical scoreline in the same competition at Tynecastle.

Hearts were in the First Division at the time but with Smith playing in every one of the 39 league games (and conceding only 39 goals), Hearts were back in the Premier Division in 1983-84.

Such was his consistency that Smith played 195 consecutive league games for Hearts between March 1982-April 1987 and he played a big part in the team's run to the verge of the league title in 1986, when he lost less than a goal a game.

Even when he did miss a game, Andy Bruce only replaced him for one fixture and then Smith embarked on an unbroken run in league and cup of 180 matches that lasted until February 2, 1991, when he lost his place after a Scottish Cup third round exit at Airdrie and Joe Jordan brought in Nicky Walker.

But Smith regained his place and played in every match in the 1991-92 season, when Hearts finished runners-up to Rangers in the league and were edged out of the Scottish Cup after a penalty shoot-out with Airdrie.

His consistency was rewarded at the end of the season, when he won his third Scottish cap against Canada (he had earlier been capped against Saudi Arabia and Northern Ireland).

Then, during a period of seemingly constant change on the managerial front at Tynecastle (Hearts had four different managers in four seasons), Smith was in and out of the team. A League Cup exit at Dens Park after a 4-4 draw was to be his last match for Hearts in September, 1995. Jim Jefferies used Craig Nelson and Gary O'Connor briefly before signing Gilles Rousset, a French international cap.

Smith, by then 39 and having been at Tynecastle for almost 15 years, was soon to leave to pursue his career at Ayr United. He had played 701 matches and set a club record of 247 clean sheets.

Born: Lanark, March 10, 1956.
Signed from: Leeds United.
Debut: August 8, 1981, League Cup, Airdrie 0 Hearts 1.
Appearances: 701.
International honours: Scotland (3).

BOBBY WALKER

It has been said that Bobby Walker is the greatest player ever to have played for Hearts. Certainly, the plaudits given to this wonderful player - and the fact that he was capped for Scotland more often (so far) than any other player wearing maroon - add weight to this argument.

His 29 caps were a record until the great Rangers winger, Alan Morton, surpassed the figure by winning a 30th cap in 1932. There is also no doubt that it was down to Walker that Hearts made their name outside of Scotland and indeed, into Europe.

Twenty-nine caps may not seem a lot when given the number that modern players can amass but it has to be remembered that in the early part of the century, Scotland were only playing internationals against England, Ireland and Wales. Walker played for Scotland for 13 years from 1900-1913 and when you consider that Scotland average at least half-a-dozen matches a year in modern times, Walker's cap total, had he played today, would probably have been around 90.

Accounts of the time suggested Walker had a deceptively slow, almost lazy, style but he was years ahead of his time and it is said he was the most perceptive of players. He had a football brain second to none at the time and his passing ability was the talk of the land. He was described as 'the father of altruistic football'.

Walker was to play a major role when Hearts captured the Scottish Cup in 1901 after beating Celtic 4-3 in a memorable final at Hampden which became known as the 'Walker final'.

Celtic were overwhelming favourites, as they were second in the league and Hearts were second-bottom. Walker, now captain, gave Hearts an early lead and after Celtic had equalised, Markie Bell put Hearts 2-1 ahead at half-time. In the second half, Walker set up Charlie Thomson for Hearts' third goal.

But Celtic came back again to level the game at 3-3 with just ten minutes left. It was Walker who steered the trophy back to Tynecastle, when his shot was saved by the Celtic goalkeeper and Bell followed up to net the winning goal.

After the match, Walker's comment to the eager press was simply, "I'd rather play than speak." But such had been his massive contribution to the game with his overall play that team-mate, Thomson, told him, "Bobby, you're the best player in Europe."

Walker was also labelled, "the greatest natural footballer who ever played"; and his fame was such that, when Hearts embarked on their first overseas tour, of Scandinavia in 1912, King Haakon of Norway turned up to watch him play in a match against Kristiana Kredslag.

Walker also played in the Hearts team that won the Scottish Cup again in 1906 with a 1-0 win over Third Lanark and again he was to play a significant role. The only goal did not arrive until nine minutes from the end, when Walker sent the ball through for George Wilson to score.

Walker was the first player to score 100 league goals for Hearts and he also had the distinction of scoring Hearts' 1,000th in league competition - against Airdrie at Tynecastle in November, 1910.

Of his 29 international caps, eleven were against England and he played nine times against Ireland and nine against Wales. He also won 14 Scottish League caps.

Born: Edinburgh, 1879.
Signed from: Dalry Primrose.
Debut: 1897.
Goals: 123 (league).
International honours: Scotland (29).

ALLAN JOHNSTON

PICTURE PROFILE

PAUL RITCHIE

aul Ritchie has come through the ranks at Tynecastle and graduated from the Scotland Schoolboys' Under-15 team to full international level.

A central defender whose ability to read the game and calm assurance belies his youth, Ritchie's worth to Hearts since signing from Links United in 1992 is difficult to overstate.

At 5'11", he is not the tallest central defender but he makes his presence felt in the air and the timing of his jump ensures that he wins more than his fair percentage of headers.

It has always been so. As a schoolboy, he gained a reputation as being a dependable and solid defender who stood head and shoulders above his peers. As a 14 year-old, he played for the Scottish Schoolboys' Under-15 team ahead of his time and it is no surprise that he has now carved out a niche in the professional game.

With a first-class attitude to the game that was evident from an early age, he can raise his game when required. He relishes the big-match atmosphere and has done well in matches against Rangers and Celtic and made his mark at international level when he headed a fine goal in a European Championship qualifier against the Czech Republic in Prague in June, 1999.

His club goals have been few and far between but he likes to come forward for set-pieces where his heading ability means he takes a lot of watching. Scored his first goal for the club in a 1-0 Scottish Cup third round win over Partick Thistle in January, 1996, and also scored in the following round's 2-1 win over Kilmarnock.

Has played alongside a number of central defenders already in his short time at Tynecastle and has adapted accordingly. Played in the 1996 Scottish Cup final against Rangers which proved a steep learning curve and gave a mature display two years later at Celtic Park when Hearts finally managed to get their hands on some silverware.

Born: Kirkcaldy, August 21, 1975.
Signed from: Links United.
Debut: September 25, 1995, Premier League: Hearts 0 Celtic 4.
Appearances: 146. Goals: 8
International honours: Scotland (2).

JIMMY WARDHAUGH

Even although John Robertson eclipsed his league scoring record for Hearts, Jimmy Wardhaugh will go down as the most consistent goalscorer in the club's history, with 376 goals in 519 matches.

Wardhaugh, born in Marshall Meadows near Berwick, was brought up in Edinburgh, where he also had a reputation as a good rugby player and cricketer before he signed for Hearts as a 17 year-old in 1946 from Shaftesbury Park. He made his debut shortly afterwards in a 3-2 win over Celtic at Tynecastle, where he scored the opening goal (Archie Kelly scored the other two).

He went on to play 11 league matches for Hearts that season and notch one more goal - in a 2-0 win over Clyde at Shawfield in the February. Hearts finished fourth in the league that season (with Kelly top scorer, on 14 goals) but Wardhaugh had already shown signs that he could make a name for himself, if not how prolific he was to be in front of goal in the years to come.

A player noted for his stamina as well as his great dribbling ability, Wardhaugh had the knack of arriving at the right place at the right time to get on the end of crosses into the penalty area.

"Jimmy was a keep-fit fanatic," points out former team-mate, John Cumming, "He could run all day and was one of the fittest players in the team. He just kept on going throughout a match; he had such a great enthusiasm for the game."

Davie McLean, the then manager, used his young forward sparingly in the early days and indeed he played only one match in 1947-48 as Hearts went through tough times and slumped to ninth in the First Division.

Wardhaugh had played a few matches with Alfie Conn but no-one could have predicted what a rich vein of goals Hearts would strike when McLean brought in a young Willie Bauld to play centre-forward in October, 1948, with Conn at inside-right and Wardhaugh at inside-left.

Curiously, Wardhaugh did not score in that infamous first match against East Fife (Bauld scored three and Conn, two) and he also failed to find the net the following week when Queen of the South were humbled, 4-0 (Bauld 3, Conn) but the goals were not long in coming. His first of that season came later in the month, when he helped Hearts beat Rangers 2-0 at Tynecastle and he went on to score ten times in the league - including a hat-trick against Albion Rovers - as Hearts crept up to eighth.

The goals were now flowing freely - Wardhaugh scored 24 in 1949-50 and in one match against Clyde, helped himself to four in a 6-2 win. But it was not until 1953-54 that he managed to finish top scorer for the club and top scorer in the division, when he amassed 34 as Hearts finished runners-up to Celtic and he handsomely outscored his colleagues, with Bauld managing only 14 and Conn 13.

He scored 27 goals in 28 league matches, most in a time when he was playing at centre-forward in place of Bauld, who had been absent through injury but by the following season, Bauld was to play a big part in Hearts' first honour for almost 50 years.

Finally, there was something tangible for Hearts to show for all these goals, as they scooped the League Cup in 1954 in a 4-2 win over Motherwell, with Bauld scoring three and Wardhaugh managing the other.

Wardhaugh led the First Division scoring again in 1955-56 with 34 goals and also claimed a Scottish Cup winners' medal, although this time there was no goal for him to celebrate in the final (Ian Crawford, 2 and Conn scored in the 3-1 win over Celtic). Twice in that season, he had scored four - against Clyde and Motherwell - and there was also a hat-trick of hat-tricks thrown in for good measure.

There were another 29 goals as Hearts finished second to Rangers the following season but it was in 1957-58 that Wardhaugh really shone, with 37 goals in all, as Hearts claimed the league title and for the third season, he was top scorer in Scotland's top league.

It is rather a misconception that it was the Terrible Trio who brought about this title success, as Bauld and Conn only played 14 league games between them. It was 26-goal Alex Young and Jimmy Murray (29 goals) who provided the back-up to Wardhaugh in all competitions that season. In the league, Hearts set a new scoring record of 132 goals.

Motherwell held the previous record of 119 from the 1930s but it was Wardhaugh who headed in Hearts' 120th of that season, in a 4-1 win over Raith Rovers at Tynecastle, to give Hearts the record. Wardhaugh also scored in the 3-2 win over St Mirren at Paisley a fortnight later that clinched the Championship for the first time in the 20th century.

There was another League Cup winners' medal for Wardhaugh in 1958 when he played - but did not score - in the 5-1 final win over Partick Thistle but this was to be his last full season at the club.

He was sold to Dunfermline for £2,000 in November, 1959, after making his last appearance for Hearts two months earlier in a 1-1 draw with Motherwell in a League Cup tie at Fir Park. His last Hearts goal was in mid-August, when he was on target in a 2-2 draw with Aberdeen at Tynecastle in the League Cup qualifying section.

The 30 year-old had lost his place to Bobby Blackwood and was thought surplus to requirements. Hearts went on to win the league without him but he had already made a considerable mark at Tynecastle, which guarantees him a prominent place in the club's history. It was not until 1997 that his club record 206 league goals was eventually overtaken by John Robertson but it has to be remembered that Wardhaugh achieved his total in just 304 league appearances, whereas Robertson's 214 goals took longer to accumulate.

Wardhaugh was to win two full caps for Scotland - in 1955, against Hungary and two years later, against Northern Ireland - which appears scant reward for his scoring exploits. He was also capped nine times for the Scottish League.

He went on to work as a sports journalist when he retired from the game. The great goalscorer died in January 1978 - on a day when Hearts were at Bayview, beating East Fife 2-1 in the First Division - at the age of only 48 and less than a year after the premature death of his centre-forward, Willie Bauld.

Born: Marshall Meadows, March 21, 1929.
Signed from: Shaftesbury Park.
Debut: August 21, 1946, First Division, Hearts 3 Celtic 2.
Appearances: 519. Goals: 376.
International honours: Scotland (2).

STEVE FULTON

PICTURE PROFILE

TOMMY WALKER

erhaps no other individual has had as big an influence on Hearts as Tommy Walker. As a player, he was respected throughout the game - north and south of the border - and as a manager, he was in charge as Hearts plundered silverware as never before. Such was his contribution that he was awarded an OBE in 1960 for his services to the game.

Born in Livingston Station, he left school at the age of 14 and two years later he joined the Hearts groundstaff. Within three years, he was commanding a regular place in the first team and had also won an international call-up for Scotland against England.

He was to go on and play 29 matches for Scotland and were it not for the Second World War, would have surely gone on to overtake the cap haul of namesake, Bobby Walker, still the most-capped Hearts player of all time.

But inside-right, Tommy Walker, was respected, not only for his ability with a football but for his sincerity and compassion. He trained for the ministry but the war intervened and he was not able to pursue the vocation.

Walker did not manage to win any honours at Tynecastle as a player but he famously scored a penalty equaliser against England at Wembley in 1936, when he kept his cool as the ball was blown off the spot three times before he slotted it past goalkeeper, Ted Sager. It gave Scotland the point they needed to win the Home International Championship. Two years later, he scored the winning goal in the corresponding fixture.

Even from an early age, Walker had shown great maturity to add to the touch and vision. His ability to score goals and lay chances on a plate for team-mates made him hugely popular with Hearts and indeed, Scotland supporters.

He returned to Hearts after the war but was to play in only eight more matches for the club before being transferred to Chelsea for a considerable £8,000 fee, after scoring 190 goals in 354 appearances during 14 years at Tynecastle.

He proved just as popular at Chelsea, where he was to spend just over two years before being lured back to Tynecastle by then manager, Davie McLean.

Billy Birrell, Chelsea's manager-secretary, summed up the player, when he wrote at the time of Walker's departure: "I doubt if any professional player has so deservedly earned such nationwide eulogies, so many complimentary adjectives, as the inimitable Tommy Walker.

"Humility is one of his outstanding characteristics - for all the heights he has attained, he has never lost his modesty. This example has been an inspiration to all with whom he comes into contact.

"If I were asked to define the true sportsman, I would unhesitatingly present Tommy as the complete example and this is the highest tribute I know."

Walker was to play only one more match for Hearts after returning in December, 1948. He played at right-half in a 1-0 defeat by Dundee, which was watched by 35,000 at Tynecastle in January, 1949.

The new manager was not to know it at the time but he inherited from McLean, players who would make Hearts arguably the best team in their history. Willie Bauld, Alfie Conn and Jimmy Wardhaugh had all been signed at modest expense and McLean had also recruited Dave Mackay, who was to have a big influence, not only on Hearts but on the British game, as a player and a manager.

There was an early indication of what Hearts fans would grow to expect, as Walker's team beat Morton 8-0 in the league, with Conn scoring a hat-trick but there was frustration the following season when Hearts lost out in the semi finals of the Scottish Cup to Motherwell after two replays.

But success was not far away. Walker guided Hearts to the League Cup Final in 1954 and - with Mackay, Bauld, Conn and Wardhaugh all in his team - they hoisted silverware for the first time in 48 years.

It was only the start. In the years that followed under Walker's management, Hearts won the League Championship twice, the Scottish Cup once and the League Cup on three more occasions. What is more, Hearts plundered the silver by playing imaginative, attacking football that won them respect throughout the land.

There were also European fields to visit and although Hearts never enjoyed too much success on this front under Walker, some of the most famous clubs in Europe found their way to Tynecastle - Standard Liege, Benfica and Inter Milan amongst them.

However, there was also to be one major disappointment, as the league title eluded Hearts in 1965, when Kilmarnock won 2-0 at Tynecastle in the league decider to pip Hearts on goal average. Walker, however, who had always stressed that the game, itself and the spirit in which it was played, was more important than winning or losing, took it all in good grace.

The following season, Hearts - understandably deflated - could finish only seventh and were knocked out in the qualifying stages of the League Cup and in the quarter finals of the Scottish Cup. Walker had become a victim of his own success after bringing seven trophies in 16 years in charge.

Walker resigned as manager in September, 1966 - his last game in charge being a 3-0 away win over Stirling Albion. There had been some unrest in the dressing-room and Walker had been informed that his position was being considered. So it was that - at the age of 52 - Walker no longer had his hand on the tiller, although he later became a director of the club in 1974 and then vice-chairman in 1979.

Walker was succeeded as manager by trainer, John Harvey, who was soon to guide Hearts to a Scottish Cup Final in 1968. But in terms of trophies, no-one could even come close to matching Walker's impressive record and indeed, it was not until 1998 that Hearts won a cup again.

Born: Livingston Station, May 26, 1915.
Signed from: Linlithgow Rose.
Debut: September 3, 1932, Division One, Hearts 4 Ayr United 2.
International honours: Scotland (20).

STEPHANE ADAM

PICTURE PROFILE

BOBBY PARKER

Bobby Parker gave a lifetime's service to Hearts as supporter, player, captain, scout, coach, director and chairman. Although born in the Borders, he moved to Bathgate with his family soon afterwards and attended his first game at Tynecastle when he was only five years old.

The six-foot defender started his playing career with Edinburgh Waverley and Bathgate Thistle and it was Partick Thistle who offered him his first senior opportunity in 1942.

Playing at centre-half, he was sure-footed in the tackle and was a player who had the ability to organise the defence into a unit. Parker's reputation soon grew. He helped Thistle win the Summer Cup in 1944-45 but he was lured to Hearts less than two years later in an exhange deal that took Jimmy Walker to Glasgow.

Parker played at right-back or right-half initially at Tynecastle but eventually made the number two slot his own after taking over from Dougal Matheson. His influence on Hearts was widely acknowledged and he was also something of a free-kick expert. Not only did he contribute in defence but he also had a knack of getting a goal or two himself.

Parker was captain of the team from 1949-56 and led Hearts to the League Cup in 1954 - the club's first major honour since 1906. He scored in the second leg of the cup quarter final against St Johnstone in a 5-0 win at Tynecastle and played in every round, before lifting the trophy on October 23, 1954, after the historic 4-2 win over Motherwell, in which Willie Bauld scored a hat-trick.

Parker was one of only three Hearts players (Fred Glidden and Jimmy Wardhaugh being the others) who played every match for the club that season.

Unfortunately, a knee injury was to rob Parker of more medals. He missed the successful Scottish Cup campaign in 1956 - when Hearts won the trophy with a 3-1 final win over Celtic - and although he made four appearances in Hearts' league title winning season of 1957-58, the injury was to force his retirement from the game at the end of that season.

He continued to represent the club in coaching and scouting capacities and became a director in 1970. He was chairman from 1974-80 and continued to serve as a director until 1993, giving great service. Always a gentleman and a thoughtful contributor both on and off the park, Parker's time at Tynecastle is fondly remembered by all who came into contact with him.

Born: Riccarton Junction, 1924.
Signed from: Partick Thistle
Debut: August 16, 1947, League Cup, Airdrie 3 Hearts 2.
Appearances: 387. Goals: 33.
International honours: 0.

ALAN McLAREN

PICTURE PROFILE

THOMAS FLOGEL

PICTURE PROFILE

BATTLES & MURRAY

PICTURE PROFILE

WILLIE BAULD WITH CUP

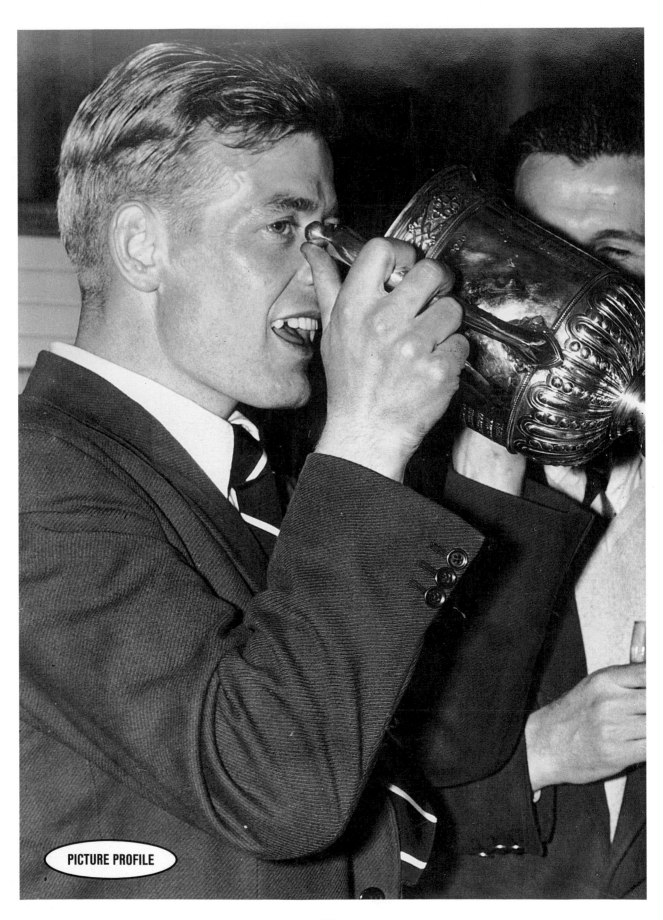

PICTURE PROFILE

NEIL McCANN & DAVID WEIR

PICTURE PROFILE